Mega Event Planning

Series Editors
Stefano Di Vita
Dipartimento Architettura Studi Urbani
Politecnico di Milano
Milano, Italy

John Lauermann
Geography
City University of New York
Cumberland, USA

The Mega Event Planning Pivot series provides a global and cross-disciplinary view into the planning for the world's largest sporting, religious, cultural, and other transformative mega events. Examples include the Olympic Games, Soccer World Cups, Rugby championships, the Commonwealth Games, the Hajj, the World Youth Day, World Expositions, and parades. This series critically discusses, analyzes, and challenges the planning for these events in light of their legacies including the built environment, political structures, socio-economic systems, societal values, personal attitudes, and cultures.

Sven Daniel Wolfe
Editor

The Hard Edge of Soft Power

Mega-Events, Geopolitics, and Making Nations Great Again

Editor
Sven Daniel Wolfe
ETH Zurich
Zürich, Switzerland

Institute of Geography
University of Neuchâtel
Neuchâtel, Switzerland

This work was supported by the Swiss National Science Foundation (SNSF).

ISSN 2633-5859 ISSN 2633-5867 (electronic)
Mega Event Planning
ISBN 978-981-96-3514-6 ISBN 978-981-96-3515-3 (eBook)
https://doi.org/10.1007/978-981-96-3515-3

The Author(s) 2025. This book is an open access publication.

Open Access This book is licensed under the terms of the Creative Commons Attribution 4.0 International License (http://creativecommons.org/licenses/by/4.0/), which permits use, sharing, adaptation, distribution and reproduction in any medium or format, as long as you give appropriate credit to the original author(s) and the source, provide a link to the Creative Commons license and indicate if changes were made.
The images or other third party material in this book are included in the book's Creative Commons license, unless indicated otherwise in a credit line to the material. If material is not included in the book's Creative Commons license and your intended use is not permitted by statutory regulation or exceeds the permitted use, you will need to obtain permission directly from the copyright holder.
The use of general descriptive names, registered names, trademarks, service marks, etc. in this publication does not imply, even in the absence of a specific statement, that such names are exempt from the relevant protective laws and regulations and therefore free for general use.
The publisher, the authors and the editors are safe to assume that the advice and information in this book are believed to be true and accurate at the date of publication. Neither the publisher nor the authors or the editors give a warranty, expressed or implied, with respect to the material contained herein or for any errors or omissions that may have been made. The publisher remains neutral with regard to jurisdictional claims in published maps and institutional affiliations.

This Palgrave Macmillan imprint is published by the registered company Springer Nature Singapore Pte Ltd.
The registered company address is: 152 Beach Road, #21-01/04 Gateway East, Singapore 189721, Singapore

If disposing of this product, please recycle the paper.

To all host city residents around the globe who lost something when the world's games came to town.

Acknowledgement

All books are collaborative efforts, but this one simply would not exist without the experts collected here. I thank every one of them, individually and as a team, for contributing such fine multidisciplinary scholarship to this broader vision. Everyone in this book does great work and I recommend you go read their other publications.

The spark for this book came from a talk I gave at Play the Game 2022 in Odense, Denmark. Titled "The Hard Edge of Soft Power", I connected the Russian mega-event decade, the inculcation of great nation narratives, and the terrible insanity of the war against Ukraine. I thank Stanis Elsborg, Jens Sejer Andersen, and the whole PtG team for giving me a prominent space to share my ideas. Afterward, it occurred to me what I saw in Russia might be part of larger patterns.

I thank Vitaly Kazakov, who invited me to give a keynote at a symposium he organized with Dmitrijs Andrejevs at the University of Manchester. Vitaly gifted me a generous time in the spotlight to develop these ideas, and his symposium is where this book started to take shape.

I thank Natalie Koch, who not only brought me to Doha—a key moment in this project—but who also has been a consistent source of encouragement and inspiration.

I thank Dennis Pauschinger for his ethical consistency and steadfast counsel in all things, from the simplest issues of water quality to the most complex inequalities at the dark heart of the Games.

I thank Allison Wagner, world champion and Olympic medalist, for sharing her story and teaching me about the athletes at the centre of the spectacle.

I thank John Lauermann for years of kindness and support. I thank Marion Duval and Karthika Devi for helping bring this project to the world. And I thank Adam Talbot, whose efforts improved this book immensely.

I also thank you for reading what we wrote.

Finally, I thank Anastassia, Sofia, and Yasha, who are everything to me.

Funding: This book was generously supported by the Swiss National Science Foundation, Ambizione Grant PZ00P1_208764

Published Open Access with the support of the Swiss National Science Foundation (SNSF). The editor and authors thank the SNSF for supporting this book and open science in general.

Competing Interests There are no competing interests.

About This Book

This book explores the linkages between geopolitics and mega-events, investigating local developments beneath the Potemkin surface of the global spectacle. From multiple perspectives and disciplines, it encompasses but also transcends the international and domestic dimensions of soft power to unpack how mega-events shape cities and societies through notions of unity and national greatness.

Drawing on a global range of case studies, this book features the sensitivity of grounded local research framed within geopolitical perspectives. It places local developments in conversation with global scales and establishes comparisons with other host cities around the world.

Chapters feature cases from Eastern Europe, Western Europe, North America, South America, Africa, the Middle East, Asia, and Australia. The authors work with a standardized conceptual toolbox established in the introduction, so the chapters speak with a coherent theoretical vocabulary regarding mega-events, soft power, geopolitics, authoritarian practices, and Potemkinism. The result is a set of contributions that harmonize with and build on each other, but nevertheless emphasize regional specificities.

Together, they combine to present an international and transdisciplinary understanding of the local and global political implications of hosting mega-events. The volume reveals what hides under the mega-event spectacle: problems that—regardless of national context—most often occur to the detriment of host populations.

Contents

1 Introduction: Rationales and Foundational Concepts 1
   Sven Daniel Wolfe

2 Geopolitics and International Sporting Events in the UK: Constitutional Navel-Gazing and the Politics of Event Hosting 19
   Stuart Whigham

3 When the Stage Came Down: A Short-Term Feel-Good Experience at South Africa's World Cup 35
   Rutendo Roselyn Musikavanhu

4 Behind the Golden Glow: The Soft Power, Potemkinism, and Protest of Australian Mega-Events 49
   Max Holleran, Jennifer Minner, and Martin Abbott

5 Stepping Out of the Shadows: The Role of Pivotal Individuals in Qatar's Aspirations to Host Mega-Events 67
   Tobias Zumbraegel and Sebastian Sons

6 From "being there is everything" to "go big or go home"? Comparing the Opening Ceremonies of the 2008 Summer Olympics and the 2022 Winter Olympics in Beijing   83
   Julia Gurol

7 The Authoritarian Legacy: Mega-Event Security, the Managerial-Militarized Model, and the Rise of the Far-Right in Brazil   97
   Bruno Cardoso and Dennis Pauschinger

8 The Eastern European Mega-Event Decade: Sports, Geopolitics, and War at the Start of the Twenty-First Century   113
   Vitaly Kazakov and Dmitrijs Andrejevs

9 The Salt Lake City 2002 Winter Olympics: Soft Power, Sportswashing, and the Invasion of Iraq   129
   Jules Boykoff and Reed McFeely

10 Conclusion: After the Spotlight   145
   Sven Daniel Wolfe

NOTES ON CONTRIBUTORS

Martin Abbott holds a Ph.D. in Science and Technology Studies from Cornell University, USA. His research interests focus on the dynamic social, environmental, and technoscientific relations that shape contemporary life, particularly in urban spaces. https://orcid.org/0000-0002-8201-6027

Dmitrijs Andrejevs is an Honorary Research Fellow at The University of Manchester, UK, and a co-convenor of the Study Group on the Baltic States under the auspices of the British Association for Slavonic and East European Studies. He holds a Ph.D. in Russian and East European Studies from the University of Manchester and was a co-organizer of the recent international symposium on "(Il)liberal Nation Projection Through Sport, Culture, Entertainment, and International Broadcasting" (20–21 October 2022) hosted at the same institution. https://orcid.org/0000-0003-3829-6161

Jules Boykoff is the author of six books on the Olympics, including *What Are the Olympics For?* (Bristol University Press, 2024); *The 1936 Berlin Olympics: Race, Power, and Sportswashing* (Common Ground, 2023); and *Power Games: A Political History of the Olympics* (Verso, 2016). He has written for academic journals such as *Sociology of Sport Journal*, the *International Journal of the History of Sport*, and the *Connecticut Journal of International Law*. He is Professor of Political Science at Pacific University, USA. https://orcid.org/0000-0002-6313-0684

Bruno Cardoso is Professor of Sociology at the Federal University of Rio de Janeiro, Brazil. Bruno has profound experience in studying police work, surveillance technologies, and state violence. His work has covered camera surveillance systems in Rio de Janeiro and the development of the mega-event security architecture. He is an active member of the Latin-American network of surveillance, technology, and society studies and is the co-founder and current coordinator of the digital studies laboratory at the Federal University of Rio de Janeiro. https://orcid.org/0000-0001-7919-1046

Julia Gurol is a postdoctoral researcher at the German Institute for Global and Area Studies. Her research focuses on China as a global actor, critical geopolitics, and China-Global South relations. Her research has been published in journals like *International Affairs*, *Journal of Contemporary China*, and *Globalizations*. Her monograph *The EU-China Security Paradox* was published with Bristol University Press in January 2022. https://orcid.org/0000-0003-4642-8013

Max Holleran is Senior Lecturer in Social Policy at the University of Melbourne, Australia. He is the author of *Yes to the City: Millennials and the Fight for Affordable Housing* (Princeton University Press, 2022) and *Tourism, Urbanization, and the Evolving Periphery of the European Union* (Palgrave, 2019). https://orcid.org/0000-0001-7177-2065

Vitaly Kazakov is a Marie Skłodowska-Curie Actions European Postdoctoral Fellow at Aarhus University, Denmark. His research interests include politics and the mediation of sport. Vitaly's new project explores the political legacies of major football tournaments in a comparative setting. He obtained his Ph.D. in Russian Studies from the University of Manchester with a study of the promotion, mediation, and reception of the Sochi 2014 Winter Olympics. Previously, he was as Lecturer in Politics at the Universities of Liverpool and Manchester, an ESRC Postdoctoral Fellow at the University of Manchester, and a RANNÍS Postdoctoral Fellow at the University of Iceland. https://orcid.org/0000-0003-1641-2598

Reed McFeely is a graduate at Pacific University, Oregon, USA. He majored in political science and philosophy. His academic work has appeared in *The International Journal of Sport and Society*. https://orcid.org/0009-0003-7974-3586

Jennifer Minner is Director of Graduate Studies and an associate professor in the Department of City and Regional Planning at Cornell University, USA. She directs the Just Places Lab, a platform for research and creative action centered on community memory, imagination, and the just care of places. https://orcid.org/0000-0002-0403-6890

Rutendo Roselyn Musikavanhu is Senior Lecturer in Event and Tourism Management in the School of Architecture + Cities at the University of Westminster, UK. Her research interests cover community support for mega-events, social impacts, legacy planning, and sustainability of events at large. https://orcid.org/0000-0003-1474-8311

Dennis Pauschinger was an Erasmus+ Fellow in the European Union Commission's EACEA Erasmus Mundus Doctorate in Cultural and Global Criminology program and associate researcher and postdoc in the Institute of Geography at the University of Neuchâtel, Switzerland. Dennis' research investigated the sociopolitical dimensions of urban security issues, digital technologies, surveillance mechanisms, and policing work during the Brazilian mega-events. He currently works as Secretary General of the Department of Construction, Energy and Environment of the City of Biel, Switzerland. https://orcid.org/0000-0002-6149-7386

Sebastian Sons works as a senior researcher for the Center for Applied Research in Partnership with the Orient (CARPO), Germany. His Ph.D. thesis dealt with media discourses on labor migration from Pakistan to Saudi Arabia. He studied Middle Eastern studies, contemporary history, and political sciences in Berlin and Damascus. His fields of interest include sport diplomacy in Saudi Arabia and Qatar, South Asian migration to the countries of the Gulf Cooperation Council (GCC), and political and economic transformations of the Gulf monarchies. He has written three books focusing on political, economic, social, and cultural developments in the GCC countries. https://orcid.org/0009-0009-1122-6455

Stuart Whigham is Senior Lecturer in Sport, Coaching, and Physical Education in the Department of Sport, Health Sciences, and Social Work at Oxford Brookes University, UK. Stuart's research interests in the sociology and politics of sport focus on national identity, nationalism, and sport; the politics of sport and sporting events; the politics of the Commonwealth Games; and the sociology and politics of Scottish sport. https://orcid.org/0000-0003-1123-2248

Sven Daniel Wolfe is Assistant Professor of Social and Cultural Geography at the University of Neuchâtel, and Swiss National Science Foundation Ambizione Fellow in the Spatial Development and Urban Policy group at the ETH Zurich, Switzerland. He works on the (geo)politics, (un)sustainability, and sociocultural implications of mega-events. He is also a vice-president of the Swiss Association of Geography, co-founder of the City Collaboratory urban studies research network, and the author of *More Than Sport: Soft Power and Potemkinism in the 2018 Men's Football World Cup in Russia* (LIT Verlag 2021). https://orcid.org/0000-0002-4517-6056

Tobias Zumbraegel is a postdoctoral researcher and lecturer in the Department for Human Geography at Heidelberg University, Germany. Prior to this, he worked at the Cluster of Excellence "Climate, Climatic Change, and Society" (CLICCS), University of Hamburg, where he is an associate fellow. He studied history, political science, and Middle Eastern studies in Cologne, Tübingen, and Cairo, and holds a Ph.D. from the Friedrich-Alexander University of Erlangen-Nuremberg. Zumbrägel is the author of *Political Power and Environmental Sustainability in Gulf Monarchies* (Palgrave 2022). https://orcid.org/0000-0002-2895-9948

CHAPTER 1

Introduction: Rationales and Foundational Concepts

Sven Daniel Wolfe

Abstract This introduction shares the book's theoretical and empirical ambitions and sets out a common conceptual ground that is employed to greater or lesser degrees by the authors of each chapter, in respect to the uniqueness of each individual case. Overall, this book is concerned with the aftereffects of hosting mega-events. It makes sense of developments around the globe through the notion of soft power, aimed both internationally and at the domestic host audience; the Potemkin relationship between spectacular but superficial promises and the deleterious outcomes that occur under that surface; and the uneasy linkages between hosting and the (geo)politics of authoritarianism and great nation populism. Each chapter highlights a different global region, featuring cases from Western Europe, Eastern Europe, Asia, the Middle East, Africa, Australia, South America, and North America. By offering a standardized conceptual toolbox in this introduction, the book presents a more coherent picture of the implications of hosting mega-events in disparate areas around the globe.

S. D. Wolfe (✉)
ETH Zürich, Zurich, Switzerland

Institute of Geography, University of Neuchâtel, Neuchâtel, Switzerland
e-mail: swolfe@ethz.ch

Keywords Soft power • Potemkinism • Geopolitics • Mega-events

Rationales

Mega-events are powerful. They have the enduring capacity to affect both individual hearts and entire nations. Billions of people love them, despite their history of damage to host cities and societies. How and why does this happen? What do they leave behind after the global spotlight moves on?

My first glimpse of the contradictions inherent in mega-events came in 2011, during a visit to relatives in London and Sochi. It was coincidence that both cities were preparing to host the upcoming Summer and Winter Olympics in 2012 and 2014. They were in frenzies of preparation and the Games were a frequent and easy topic wherever I went. From afar, I had thought that preparing to host the Olympics would be breathlessly exciting in the host city, all glamor and anticipation. I still remember the surprise of hearing how many residents actually felt.

Instead of the popular support I expected, I found apathy, frustration, or outright disdain for the Games. I began recording conversations to preserve this seeming paradox. Listening now, over a decade later, two quotations stand out:

> "I'm absolutely not staying [in 2012]. ... It's already mad here and next summer it'll be impossible. Not a chance."
> —North London resident, 2011

> "It's non-stop construction, you can't imagine. ... But if they fulfil their promises, if they just provide us with gas, then we'll forgive everything."
> —Sochi region village resident, 2011

These snippets reveal some of the everyday realities that hide under the mega-event spectacle. In London, the resident was complaining about Olympic-related disruptions to her commute and working life. It was already difficult for her in the preparatory period, so the idea of staying in London during the actual Games seemed unendurable. She unabashedly shared her plans to escape the coming chaos. Her neighbors felt similarly and, with a mixture of exasperation and pride, they traded ideas of where they should go during summer 2012. It felt natural to leave the country for this well-to-do set, and there was no mention of support for Team GB.

Living in a relatively underserved mountain village, the Sochi resident had similar complaints about disruption, though hers were grounded in more foundational problems. Previously, the string of villages between the two new clusters of Olympic venues were quiet, rural, and removed from the bustle of the urban coast. Poorly connected to municipal infrastructure, villagers were accustomed to a certain self-reliance. Power outages were common and repairs were slow. Water came from a local well with an unreliable pump, so those who could afford it kept backup cisterns of non-potable water. There was no gas connection, so villagers heated their houses with wood or coal, and cooked with propane in tanks they replaced themselves. For all that, complaints were few. This was the way it had always been.

Once the Olympics were announced, however, the atmosphere changed. Local authorities pledged to harness the development energies of the Games and improve quality of life for everyone. They promised paved roads, connections to a new highway, stable electricity, potable water, and gas. In the first years after the announcement, I saw alienation and cynicism give way to hope—particularly as authorities shared concrete plans for improvements. But by 2011, already four years into the preparations, there were no improvements for locals. Instead, maximum effort was being poured into the mega-event, building an entirely new tourist town around the mountain cluster of venues. Construction was constant, loud, dusty, and dangerous. Enormous open-bed trucks roared up and down the mountain at all hours. Relentless jackhammering echoed through the valley and at night the spotlights for the workers blotted out the stars. None of the promised improvements had come to pass (see Wolfe, 2020a, 2025, for more on Olympic-led development in these villages). For the woman quoted here, hosting the Olympics was not about sport or national pride, but about bringing basic material provisioning to her everyday life and enduring upheaval until that day arrived. The drilling put so much broken rock into the air that she dusted her windowsills four times a day.

Given this history, I was floored by the profound transformation of attitudes once the Olympics began. During my next UK visit, I learned that the same North London crowd had completely altered their perception of the Games. They were happy and proud—not only of hosting and sport but also of their city and nation. They did not recall wanting to leave London, and instead seemed almost smug that their city had hosted and their athletes had triumphed. This Olympic afterglow was the positive psycho-social impact, the "feel-good factor" that makes mega-event hosting such a draw for political figures and leaders the world over (Hiller & Wanner, 2015). It is potent stuff.

I found similar emotional patterns in Sochi, where I gathered with relatives and friends around the living room television to watch the Opening Ceremony (who among ordinary people could afford tickets?). It was remarkable to watch the televised spectacle melt away their years of frustration. Without exaggeration, the ceremony moved people to tears—and no one remembered the lack of gas or the dozen other broken promises and Olympic-related disasters. I witnessed the magic of the feel-good factor in real-time, shifting the hearts of people who had suffered and were continuing to suffer because of Olympic-led development.

Naturally, this euphoria could not last. It began to fade soon after the Closing Ceremony, leaving what could be called the mega-event hangover (Hall & Hodges, 1996). Like the regrets that follow an evening of overindulgence, the "morning after" a mega-event too often comprises a dawning recognition of the many planning and management disasters that occurred during the pressures of the preparations. These problems are well-documented in mega-events around the globe and include underestimated costs, busted budgets, oversized and unnecessary infrastructures, and a variety of other deleterious social, political, ecological, and economic impacts (Flyvbjerg et al., 2021; Karamichas, 2013; Müller, 2015a). They are universal, though their severity varies. Examining mega-events after the spotlight reveals that broken promises are less an exception and more of a rule.

Regardless of nation or political-economic context, the mega-event story remains largely the same: a preparatory phase filled with promises and then disruptions, an event phase where the feel-good effect works its magic, and a hang-over phase where the actual impacts come to light—by which time most media and scholarly attention has moved on to the next Games down the list. The promises of economic booms, urban revitalization, increased participation in sport, environmental progress, and any of the many meanings of "sustainability" achieve limited or selective successes at best, and at worst are outright deceptive and destructive (Baade & Matheson, 2004; Horne & Whannel, 2016; Mair et al., 2023; Müller et al., 2021; Weaver et al., 2021). Typically, mega-events succeed at spectacle but at little else. In many ways they are classic examples of Potemkinism, where a superficial surface masks less savory realities underneath (Broudehoux, 2017; Wolfe, 2021, 2023).

Yet there is more to the story than this. Alongside the too-familiar tales of broken promises, marginalization, displacement, destruction, and loss, the feel-good factor can have real implications on cities and societies. Sometimes fleeting but sometimes durable, the social dimension of mega-events is all at once subjective but real, artificial but authentic. Often, it is one of the only positive aftereffects of hosting (Cornelissen & Maennig, 2010; Musikavanhu et al., 2021; J. Sugden & Tomlinson, 1996). At the same time, the feel-good factor is not necessarily innocent: it can be created, coopted, or instrumentalized. It can be shaped by state actors for (geo)political purposes.

One of the goals of this book is to explore the political implications of hosting mega-events across a range of cases from around the globe, combining the sensitivity of grounded local research with broader perspectives on geopolitics and global affairs. Each chapter comprises a unique case, where the articulation of the event is contingent on the host country's specific national, cultural, political, and economic contexts. But mega-events are also global productions, enrolled in and dependent on dense translocal networks. Thus, local processes are enmeshed with broader regional and international developments. Each mega-event is simultaneously hyperlocal and in deep conversation with the wider world.

Against the backdrop of the mega-event story (preparatory phase of promises and disruptions, event phase with the power of the feel-good factor, and hang-over phase of realization and regret), the chapters collected here unpack some of the paradoxes of mega-events (Müller, 2017). In so doing, they uncover the (geo)political ramifications of hosting at a variety of scales, and from the vantage point of multiple academic disciplines and traditions. They begin from a common concern for the everyday impacts that continue to affect host cities and societies after the global spotlight has moved on.

Foundational Concepts

This is a collective work composed by an international and multidisciplinary team of experts, all of whom have unique expertise in their regions. To avoid the disjointed character that sometimes plagues edited volumes, the authors work with the same basic theoretical vocabulary, introduced here. This conceptual foundation remains consistent throughout the book, meaning that each chapter is relatively shorter, more empirical, and with less theoretical background than might be expected in a more traditional academic endeavor. The aim is to spare the reader the redundancy and potential confusion of parsing different authors' particular conceptual engagements. Each author or author team engages with the book's foundational concepts to whatever degree they wish and follows their cases to their own conclusions, but the overall goal is the same: to engage similar tools to explore the (geo)political implications of hosting mega-events at a range of scales, from the individual to the global.

We begin with the basic definition of mega-events. These hallmarks of modernity are short-term, one-off celebrations of sport or culture that cost and generate fortunes, attract global attention, and engender long-term impacts on cities and societies (Horne, 2007; Müller, 2015b; Roche, 2002). They are inseparable from international and domestic politics, and are the perennially popular subject of a global and interdisciplinary academic literature (Bairner et al., 2017; Cornelissen, 2010; Koch, 2017). This literature has some problems, however: first, most scholarly and media attention occurs during the preparatory phases, and there is a tendency to forget host cities after the Closing Ceremony, when global attention shifts to the next Games down the list. Work on the aftereffects of hosting—even simply following up on the promises from the preparatory period—is too rare. This book returns past mega-events to the spotlight.

To be sure, there is some literature on mega-event legacy, a term that refers broadly to a host-city's post-event condition. Despite the fact that it appears in some chapters here, I personally prefer to avoid the term because of its conceptual fuzziness: organizers and boosters employ it in an exclusively positive sense, while scholars tend toward a more heterogeneous and sometimes critical view (Koenigstorfer et al., 2019; Leopkey & Parent, 2012). For me, the crucial aspect is to acknowledge that "legacy" is contested and using it risks contributing to a normative positive framing that presents hosting experiences as an unalloyed good for all (see Wolfe et al., 2024 for more on this and other contested terms). Instead, I endeavor to frame the lingering impacts of mega-event hosting as *aftereffects*, which carry less conceptual and ideological baggage. My hope would be that work on mega-event aftereffects does justice to actually existing complexities, while also reminding global audiences of the importance of remembering and contextualizing with previous host cities and societies. Regardless of terminology, the fact remains that for all their global attention, mega-events—and especially the host city population—largely disappear from public attention after the Games leave town.

Another problem in the mega-events literature is that most of the field is composed of single case studies. The comparative studies that do exist focus on a given aspect, such as economic impact or urban development, or tracking a certain definition of legacy or sustainability (Chalkley & Essex, 1999; Fett, 2020; Leonardsen, 2007; Leopkey & Parent, 2012; Müller et al., 2021). This book is similar: we begin in the general domain of mega-event politics, investigating how hosting shapes individuals and societies through notions of unity and greatness, but also unpacking local developments underneath the Potemkin surface of the global spectacle (Broudehoux, 2015; Wolfe, 2023). The book aspires to present the best of both worlds: in-depth case studies built on local expertise, but framed in global comparative perspective in order to bring larger patterns and new conclusions to light.

The notion of mega-event politics is broad and diverse. A political framing has been engaged to study the governance of sporting institutions, the marriage of sport and ideology, how sport influences notions of ethnicity and statehood, and the intersections of global sport and modernity (Bairner et al., 2017; Black, 2007; Boykoff, 2016; Roche, 2002). Another common usage of the political is to explore the mechanisms and rationales that underpin hosting mega-events, and the implications that follow on a variety of publics. In this context, work can be divided roughly into domestic and international strands.

Domestically, work tends to focus on the politics of hosting coalitions, the local articulations of urban planning, the repercussions of surveillance and securitization processes, and popular resistance (Dart & Wagg, 2016; Giulianotti & Klauser, 2011; Hiller, 2000; Lauermann, 2014; Lauermann & Vogelpohl, 2017; Pauschinger, 2023). Internationally, work centers on the so-called global stage, framing mega-events as a tool of statecraft, international relations, or sports diplomacy (Grix, 2015; Nygård & Gates, 2013; Pamment, 2019; Postlethwaite et al., 2023). This can also be understood as mega-event geopolitics (Koch, 2017).

This geopolitics of mega-events is often conceptualized as part of a nation's soft power toolbox (Nye, 1990, 2005, 2008), where soft power is the ability of states to achieve goals not through military or economic force, but by the politics of attraction and cooptation. It is about "getting others to want what you want" (Nye, 1990, p. 167). In the context of mega-events, soft power is understood either to introduce a new understanding of the host nation to the global stage or to launder the national image through sport (Boykoff, 2022; Grix & Brannagan, 2016; Jeong,

2021). More specifically, soft power has been used to explain the hosting aspirations for the new generation of mega-event nations outside of the Global North. In this reading, hosting mega-events is a way for "new" or "developing" nations to claim a place alongside major states, to leverage image politics on the global stage, and to open up to international flows of attention, tourists, and capital (Black & Westhuizen, 2004; Cornelissen, 2010; Grix et al., 2019).

Not every nation can secure hosting rights for the Olympics or the men's Football World Cup, however, so the supposed soft power benefits of the world's most prestigious mega-events remain out of reach. For these, there exist a range of second- and third-tier options that nevertheless have the potential to engender similar—although smaller-scale—effects. These aspirational events remain understudied in comparison to their larger and more famous cousins. Addressing this oversight, some authors collected in this volume bring them into conversation with better-known mega-events. For instance, see Whigham on the 2014 Commonwealth Games in Glasgow; Holleran, Minner, and Abbott on Expo '88 in Brisbane; Zumbraegel and Sons on COP18 in Qatar; and Kazakov and Andrejevs on middle-tier mega-events in Central and Eastern Europe. The potential of soft power gains for various audiences plays a key role in all of these events.

In general, the literature on mega-event soft power tends to show a bias toward global scales, reflecting the concept's origins in political science and international relations. A major problem, however, is that this view overlooks the host population. Thus, another rationale for this book is that any instrumentalization of soft power that neglects the domestic is incomplete. To be sure, there exists a separate body of good work that explores the domestic implications of mega-event hosting, generally framing developments through nation-building, identity formation, and symbolic politics (e.g., Alekseyeva, 2014; Kazakov, 2019; Koch, 2013; Militz, 2019; Whigham, 2022). I submit that this domestically focused literature could gain by considering the conceptual vocabulary of soft power. Including domestic populations as a target audience for soft power brings new light to the relationships between state actors, mega-event coalitions, and host populations. This helps us read mega-events within the broader story of a city and nation's unique trajectory.

I explored domestic soft power previously (e.g., Wolfe, 2016, 2021), but for the purposes of this book, the theoretical approach in Wolfe (2020b) is most relevant. There, I theorized soft power along several dimensions. In my reading, soft power is not just a tool of official statecraft, but can be created or coopted by multiple agents simultaneously. This perspective acknowledges that different actors with potentially conflicting goals can attempt to harness mega-events for their own designs. Further, institutional actors themselves are not monolithic, and can contain multitudes of differing aspirations. This end of the soft power equation, then, is more complex than traditionally recognized, comprising a heterogeneous assemblage of organizers, local and national authorities, event franchise owners, and domestic and international business concerns, each with their own internal divisions and external postures. This complexity has implications on how soft power is conceived of, formed, engaged, and directed.

It gets more complicated: it is not just soft power creators that are multiple, but also soft power targets. In much of the literature, the audience for soft power projects is assumed to be both international and singular. This is dangerously reductionist. There is an unstated assumption in much of Nye's foundational work—and subsequently much of the work he inspired—that the North American experience and perspective is the default. This perspective misses the breadth and diversity of the global population, and behaves as though the only potential audience for a nation's soft power aspirations must be the United States (or more charitably the Global North or "The West"). In truth, when nations outside of Western Europe and North America host mega-events, they direct significant energies toward a multitude of other audiences, especially in the so-called Global South, as detailed in this volume by Zumbraegel and Sons with Qatar; by Gurol regarding Beijing; and by Kazakov and Andrejevs in reference to the nations of Central and Eastern Europe. Soft power is messy and multiple.

Moreover, soft power exists in dynamic interplay with hard power, where hard power is understood as the coercion of economic or military force. In later work, Nye attempted to balance these supposed opposites, working with what he called *smart power* (Nye, 2011). In Nye's reading, a state's successful smart power strategy integrates all available resources to achieve policy goals. In contrast, the work collected here demonstrates how hard power realities act as both context and constraint for soft power projects. As much as authorities may wish to leverage mega-events to present a friendly and welcoming image to the wider world, these aspirations are always undergirded by a lurking undercurrent of violence and the relentless pursuit of profit. This is the hard edge of soft power.

Finally, there is another factor that is commonly overlooked: the issue of time. As soft power is not singular, neither is it stable. Instead, it shifts over time due to a variety of factors, including the vagaries of political-economic context and the demands of hard power. A nation that bids for and wins mega-event hosting rights is, in many ways, different from the nation that actually hosts. The shifting constellations of power and personal relationships have implications for how soft power is both understood and articulated. Soft power is fluid, complex, multiple, subjective, operates differently at different scales, intermingles with hard power, and changes over time.

It is important to note that this book's engagement with soft power is not an attempt to nail down this famously fluid and ambiguous concept (Brannagan & Giulianotti, 2023; Feklyunina, 2016). Nor is it relevant here to consider the nuanced overlaps and divergences between soft power, nation branding, public diplomacy, or sports diplomacy (Rookwood, 2019). In point of fact, an argument could be made that the notion of soft power obscures more than it reveals, and probably has outlived its conceptual utility. Still, the term continues to be used by scholars and practitioners alike, so we employ it here too, particularly as it continues to have relevance outside of the academy. Rather than a concern with soft power itself, however, the point here is to focus on soft power's hard edge, and to use this as an entry point to explore the mega-event Potemkin dynamic between spectacular promises and damaging outcomes. This book is concerned with the interplay between soft and hard powers, and in the mega-event gap between rhetoric and reality.

Potemkinism is predicated on the relationship between a beautiful but superficial surface that hides a less palatable reality underneath (Broudehoux, 2015, 2017; Wolfe, 2023). There are overlaps between mega-event Potemkinism and Debord's work on spectacle (see Tomlinson, 2002), but the concepts are distinct. Grounded in Marxian thought, Debord's spectacle refers to alienation, the loss of authenticity through commodification, the colonization of everyday life, and the suppression of critical thought. In contrast, Potemkinism—predating Marx by several decades—stems from the voyage of Empress Catherine II to the conquered territories of Novorossiya and Crimea, and the apocryphal story of Prince Grigory Potemkin tricking her with fake village façades along the river banks (Panchenko, 1999). The concept is less about commodification and capital accumulation than it is about managed artifice for an event, especially regarding the concealment of poverty, damage, and decay. Engaging the concept of Potemkinism is useful for disrupting the typical chronology of the mega-event story, puncturing the power of the feel-good factor, and bringing to light damages that normally only become visible during the hang-over phase of realization and regret. It is also a way to render visible those host city residents who lost something when the Games came to town, and whose problems are too often drowned out by the glare of the spectacle. This is the tactic engaged by Musikavanhu in her chapter on South Africa 2010, diving under the Potemkin surface to focus on overlooked residents.

A final example of Potemkinism stems from the sale of broadcasting rights—the source of most mega-event profits. This requires a manicured presentation of the host city that is palatable for global business, yet the situation for residents often differs wildly from the sanitized view beamed around the globe. The mega-event city looks fabulous, and indeed is a marvelous party for some, but in actuality the true costs and impacts are concealed.

Beyond soft power and Potemkinism, there are a few more themes at play in this book. Notably, mega-events have expanded beyond the traditional hosts in the Global North, leading to investigations of the overlaps between mega-events and authoritarianism. This was expressed memorably in 2013 by Jèrôme Valcke, then FIFA Secretary General, when he said:

> I will say something crazy, but less democracy is sometimes better for organizing a World Cup. When you have a very strong head of state who can decide, as maybe Putin can do in 2018, that is easier for us organizers than a country such as Germany. (quoted in Reuters, 2013)

With refreshing candor, Valcke explains why organizers appreciate authoritarian or authoritarian-leaning countries, and reveals some of the fundamental contradictions and hypocrisies involved in the current model of hosting mega-events. In the final analysis, and regardless of politics or sport or emotion, this is a multi-billion-dollar business. Valcke's logic is coherent: FIFA is not in the business of democracy or sustainability or positive legacies or the other platitudes commonly used by organizers and boosters. FIFA is in the business of making money from a sport that is so colossally popular that it has been called the world's religion. If an authoritarian politics helps ensure the security of the business, then that can only be an advantage. The logic of the profit motive does not necessarily agree with authentic democratic processes (though see Fett, 2019 for an economic analysis of the benefits of more democratic hosts).

There are serious problems with classifying nations whole cloth as authoritarian or not, however. Here, we focus not on authoritarian *states*, but authoritarian *practices* (Glasius, 2018a, 2018b). This perspective eschews the notion that nations are discrete containers ready for labeling, and rather allows for the discovery and analysis of authoritarian actions—including in host countries that might otherwise be classified as democratic. This opens a new dimension in the mega-events literature, particularly when brought into conversation with the conceptual vocabulary of domestic soft power. Here, the risk is that the spectacular emotional and affective power of hosting a mega-event can introduce or entrench political practices and technologies that are detrimental to democratic politics and human rights, as detailed here by Cardoso and Pauschinger in Brazil, Kazakov and Andrejevs in Russia, and Boykoff and McFeely in the United States. Mega-event soft power can be directed toward domestic audiences to generate great nation populist narratives that are later shaped for nefarious (geo)political purposes.

Further, focusing on practices helps avoid the orientalization or outright racism that can occur when discussing mega-event hosts outside of the Global North. This is not an argument to avoid criticism, but rather a move against essentialism, and to an understanding that non-democratic practices and deleterious outcomes can occur everywhere. These are global problems that manifest in local contexts, shaped by local conditions, but they are not unique to a particular area of the globe.

On this conceptual foundation, this book presents chapters on mega-events in Eastern Europe, Western Europe, North America, South America, Africa, the Middle East, Asia, and Australia. Though the chapters engage with all the foundational concepts to various degrees, they are ordered here around their primary themes. Chapters 2 (Whigham: United Kingdom), 3 (Musikavanhu: South Africa), and 4 (Holleran, Minner, and Abbott: Australia), all center on the Potemkin dynamic. Chapter 5 (Zumbraegel and Sons: Qatar) also explores Potemkinism but continues into authoritarian functioning. Chapters 6 (Gurol: China) and 7 (Cardoso and Pauschinger: Brazil) focus largely on authoritarian practices. Chapter 8 (Kazakov and Andrejevs: Central and Eastern Europe) continues the authoritarian discussion but moves into hard power, and Chap. 9 (Boykoff and McFeely: United States) finishes on the interplay between power soft and hard. Finally, in Chap. 10, I identify patterns between the chapters, draw conclusions, and suggest some potential directions for future research.

Bringing diverse global cases into conversation, the book encompasses and transcends the international and domestic dimensions of mega-events, allowing space for regional specificities while remembering developments at larger scales. We bring past events back to the spotlight, exploring the forgotten spaces between Potemkin rhetoric and lived reality, and unpacking the aftereffects of what actually happens to cities and societies when mega-events come to town.

References

Alekseyeva, A. (2014). Sochi 2014 and the rhetoric of a new Russia: Image construction through mega-events. *East European Politics, 30*(2), 158–174. https://doi.org/10.1080/21599165.2013.877710

Baade, R., & Matheson, V. (2004). The quest for the cup: Assessing the economic impact of the World Cup. *Regional Studies, 38*(4), 343–354. https://doi.org/10.1080/03434002000213888

Bairner, A., Kelly, J., & Lee, J. W. (2017). *Routledge handbook of sport and politics.* Routledge.

Black, D. (2007). The symbolic politics of sport mega-events: 2010 in comparative perspective. *Politikon, 34*(3), 261–276. https://doi.org/10.1080/02589340801962536

Black, D., & Westhuizen, J. V. D. (2004). The allure of global games for 'semiperipheral' polities and spaces: A research agenda. *Third World Quarterly, 25*(7), 1195–1214. https://doi.org/10.1080/014365904200281221

Boykoff, J. (2016). *Power games: A political history of the Olympics.* Verso Books.

Boykoff, J. (2022). Toward a theory of sportswashing: Mega-events, soft power, and political conflict. *Sociology of Sport Journal, 39*(4), 342–351. https://doi.org/10.1123/ssj.2022-0095

Brannagan, P. M., & Giulianotti, R. (2023). Unlocking the whole of soft power: A quantum international relations analysis. *Journal of Political Power, 16*(3), 301–321. https://doi.org/10.1080/2158379X.2023.2270412

Broudehoux, A.-M. (2015). Mega-events, urban image construction, and the politics of exclusion. In R. Gruneau & J. Horne (Eds.), *Mega-events and globalization* (Vol. 1, pp. 113–130). Routledge. https://doi.org/10.4324/9781315752174-14

Broudehoux, A.-M. (2017). *Mega-events and urban image construction : Beijing and Rio de Janeiro.* Routledge. https://doi.org/10.4324/9781315393308

Chalkley, B., & Essex, S. (1999). Urban development through hosting international events: A history of the Olympic Games. *Planning Perspectives, 14*(4), 369–394. https://doi.org/10.1080/026654399364184

Cornelissen, S. (2010). The geopolitics of global aspiration: Sport mega-events and emerging powers. *The International Journal of the History of Sport*, *27*(16–18), 3008–3025. https://doi.org/10.1080/09523367.2010.508306

Cornelissen, S., & Maennig, W. (2010). On the political economy of 'feel-good' effects at sport mega-events: Experiences from FIFA Germany 2006 and prospects for South Africa 2010. *Alternation*, *17*(2), 96–120.

Dart, J., & Wagg, S. (2016). *Sport, protest and globalisation: Stopping play*. Springer.

Feklyunina, V. (2016). Soft power and identity: Russia, Ukraine and the 'Russian world(s)'. *European Journal of International Relations*, *22*(4), 773–796. https://doi.org/10.1177/1354066115601200

Fett, M. (2019). More democracy is better for organising a World Cup. *Play the Game*. Retrieved August 31, 2023, from https://www.playthegame.org/news/more-not-less-democracy-is-often-better-for-organising-a-world-cup/

Fett, M. (2020). The game has changed—A systematic approach to classify FIFA World Cups. *International Journal of Sport Policy and Politics*, *12*(3), 455–470. https://doi.org/10.1080/19406940.2020.1784978

Flyvbjerg, B., Budzier, A., & Lunn, D. (2021). Regression to the tail: Why the Olympics blow up. *Environment and Planning A: Economy and Space*, *53*(2), 233–260. https://doi.org/10.1177/0308518X20958724

Giulianotti, R., & Klauser, F. (2011). Introduction: Security and surveillance at sport mega events. *Urban Studies*, *48*(15), 3157–3168. https://doi.org/10.1177/0042098011422400

Glasius, M. (2018a). What authoritarianism is … and is not:* A practice perspective. *International Affairs*, *94*(3), 515–533. https://doi.org/10.1093/ia/iiy060

Glasius, M. (2018b). Extraterritorial authoritarian practices: A framework. *Globalizations*, *15*(2), 179–197. https://doi.org/10.1080/14747731.2017.1403781

Grix, J. (2015). *Sport politics: An introduction* (1st ed.). Red Globe Press.

Grix, J., & Brannagan, P. M. (2016). Of mechanisms and myths: Conceptualising states' "Soft Power" strategies through sports mega-events. *Diplomacy & Statecraft*, *27*(2), 251–272. https://doi.org/10.1080/09592296.2016.1169791

Grix, J., Brannagan, P. M., & Lee, D. (2019). *Entering the global arena: Emerging states, soft power strategies and sports mega-events*. Palgrave Pivot. https://doi.org/10.1007/978-981-13-7952-9

Hall, C. M., & Hodges, J. (1996). The party's great, but what about the hangover?: The housing and social impacts of mega-events with special reference to the 2000 Sydney Olympics. *Festival Management and Event Tourism*, *4*(1–2), 13–20. https://doi.org/10.3727/106527096792232414

Hiller, H. (2000). Mega-events, urban boosterism and growth strategies: An analysis of the objectives and legitimations of the Cape Town 2004 Olympic bid.

International Journal of Urban and Regional Research, 24(2), 449–458. https://doi.org/10.1111/1468-2427.00256

Hiller, H., & Wanner, R. (2015). The psycho-social impact of the Olympics as urban festival: A leisure perspective. *Leisure Studies, 34*(6), 672–688. https://doi.org/10.1080/02614367.2014.986510

Horne, J. (2007). The four 'Knowns' of sports mega-events. *Leisure Studies, 26*(1), 81–96. https://doi.org/10.1080/02614360500504628

Horne, J., & Whannel, G. (2016). *Understanding the Olympics*. Routledge.

Jeong, J. (2021). *How nations use sport mega-events to leverage soft power: A new rise in East Asia*. Doctoral. Manchester Metropolitan University. https://e-space.mmu.ac.uk/627506/

Karamichas, J. (2013). *The Olympic games and the environment*. Palgrave Macmillan. https://link.springer.com/book/10.1057/9781137297471

Kazakov, V. (2019, December 11). *Representations of 'New Russia' through a 21st century mega-event: The political aims, informational means, and popular reception of the Sochi 2014 winter Olympic Games* (Doctoral). University of Manchester, Manchester. Retrieved from https://research.manchester.ac.uk/en/publications/representations-of-new-russia-through-a-21st-century-mega-event-t

Koch, N. (2013). Sport and soft authoritarian nation-building. *Political Geography, 32*, 42–51. https://doi.org/10.1016/j.polgeo.2012.11.006

Koch, N. (Ed.). (2017). *Critical geographies of sport: Space, power and sport in global perspective*. Routledge.

Koenigstorfer, J., Bocarro, J. N., Byers, T., Edwards, M. B., Jones, G. J., & Preuss, H. (2019). Mapping research on legacy of mega sporting events: Structural changes, consequences, and stakeholder evaluations in empirical studies. *Leisure Studies, 38*(6), 729–745. https://doi.org/10.1080/02614367.2019.1662830

Lauermann, J. (2014). Competition through interurban policy making: Bidding to host megaevents as entrepreneurial networking. *Environment and Planning A, 46*(11), 2638–2653. https://doi.org/10.1068/a130112p

Lauermann, J., & Vogelpohl, A. (2017). Fragile growth coalitions or powerful contestations? Cancelled Olympic bids in Boston and Hamburg. *Environment and Planning A: Economy and Space, 49*(8), 1887–1904. https://doi.org/10.1177/0308518X17711447

Leonardsen, D. (2007). Planning of mega events: Experiences and lessons. *Planning Theory & Practice, 8*(1), 11–30. https://doi.org/10.1080/14649350601158105

Leopkey, B., & Parent, M. M. (2012). Olympic games legacy: From general benefits to sustainable long-term legacy. *The International Journal of the History of Sport, 29*(6), 924–943. https://doi.org/10.1080/09523367.2011.623006

Mair, J., Chien, P. M., Kelly, S. J., & Derrington, S. (2023). Social impacts of mega-events: A systematic narrative review and research agenda. *Journal of*

Sustainable Tourism, 31(2), 538–560. https://doi.org/10.1080/0966958 2.2020.1870989

Militz, E. (2019). *Affective nationalism: Bodies, materials and encounters with the Nation in Azerbaijan*. LIT Verlag. Retrieved January 4, 2021.

Müller, M. (2015a). The mega-event syndrome: Why so much goes wrong in mega-event planning and what to do about it. *Journal of the American Planning Association, 81*(1), 6–17. https://doi.org/10.1080/01944363.2015.1038292

Müller, M. (2015b). What makes an event a mega-event? Definitions and sizes. *Leisure Studies, 34*(6), 627–642. https://doi.org/10.1080/0261436 7.2014.993333

Müller, M. (2017). Approaching paradox: Loving and hating mega-events. *Tourism Management, 63*, 234–241. https://doi.org/10.1016/j.tourman.2017.06.003

Müller, M., Wolfe, S. D., Gaffney, C., Gogishvili, D., Hug, M., & Leick, A. (2021). An evaluation of the sustainability of the Olympic Games. *Nature Sustainability, 4*(4), 340–348. https://doi.org/10.1038/s41893-021-00696-5

Musikavanhu, R. R., Ladkin, A., & Sadd, D. (2021). The lasting social value of mega events: Experiences from green point community in Cape Town, South Africa. *Journal of Sustainable Tourism, 29*(11–12), 1832–1849. https://doi.org/10.1080/09669582.2021.1874395

Nye, J. S. (1990). Soft power. *Foreign Policy, 80*, 153–171. https://doi.org/10.2307/1148580

Nye, J. S. (2005). *Soft power: The means to success in world politics* (New ed.). PublicAffairs.

Nye, J. S. (2008). Public diplomacy and soft power. *The Annals of the American Academy of Political and Social Science, 616*(1), 94–109. https://doi.org/10.1177/0002716207311699

Nye, J. S. (2011). *The future of power* (1st ed.). PublicAffairs.

Nygård, H. M., & Gates, S. (2013). Soft power at home and abroad: Sport diplomacy, politics and peace-building. *International Area Studies Review, 16*(3), 235–243. https://doi.org/10.1177/2233865913502971

Pamment, J. (2019). Special issue on sports diplomacy. *Place Branding and Public Diplomacy, 15*(3), 145–146. https://doi.org/10.1057/s41254-019-00136-4

Panchenko, A. (1999). 'Potemkinskie derevni' kak kulturnyi mif ['Potemkin villages' as cultural myth]. In *Russkaya istoriya i kultura: rabota raznikh let [Russian history and culture: A work of various years]* (pp. 462–475). Yuna. Retrieved March 20, 2019, from http://ec-dejavu.ru/p/Potemkin_village.html

Pauschinger, D. (2023). The triangle of security governance: Sovereignty, discipline and the 'government of things' in Olympic Rio de Janeiro. *Security Dialogue, 54*(1), 94–111. https://doi.org/10.1177/09670106221142142

Postlethwaite, V., Jenkin, C., & Sherry, E. (2023). Sport diplomacy: An integrative review. *Sport Management Review, 26*(3), 361–382. https://doi.org/10.1080/14413523.2022.2071054

Reuters. (2013, April 24). Soccer: Less democracy makes for an easier World Cup - Valcke. *Reuters.* Retrieved August 31, 2023, from https://www.reuters.com/article/us-soccer-fifa-idUSBRE93N18F20130424

Roche, M. (2002). *Mega-events and modernity: Olympics and expos in the growth of global culture.* Taylor & Francis.

Rookwood, J. (2019). Access, security and diplomacy: Perceptions of soft power, nation branding and the organisational challenges facing Qatar's 2022 FIFA World Cup. *Sport, Business and Management: An International Journal, 9*(1), 26–44. https://doi.org/10.1108/SBM-02-2018-0016

Sugden, J., & Tomlinson, A. (1996). What's left when the circus leaves town? An evaluation of World Cup USA 1994. *Sociology of Sport Journal, 13*(3), 238–258. https://doi.org/10.1123/ssj.13.3.238

Tomlinson, A. (2002). Theorising spectacle: Beyond Debord. In J. P. Sugden & A. Tomlinson (Eds.), *Power games: A critical sociology of sport* (pp. 44–60). Routledge.

Weaver, D., Moyle, B. D., & McLennan, C. (2021). A core/periphery perspective on mega-event sustainability: Dystopic and utopic scenarios. *Tourism Management, 86,* 104340. https://doi.org/10.1016/j.tourman.2021.104340

Whigham, S. (2022). Bannockburn, Braveheart, or Baccara? Ethnosymbolism, nationalism, and sport in contemporary Scotland. *National Identities, 0*(0), 1–18. https://doi.org/10.1080/14608944.2022.2147493

Wolfe, S. D. (2016). A silver medal project: The partial success of Russia's soft power in Sochi 2014. *Annals of Leisure Research, 19*(4), 481–496. https://doi.org/10.1080/11745398.2015.1122534

Wolfe, S. D. (2020a). A new road and rail link from the mountains to the coast: The mixed legacy of Sochi's most expensive project. In G. Evans (Ed.), *Mega-events: Placemaking, regeneration and city-regional development* (pp. 106–123). https://doi.org/10.4324/9780429466595-7

Wolfe, S. D. (2020b). 'For the benefit of our nation': Unstable soft power in the 2018 men's World Cup in Russia. *International Journal of Sport Policy and Politics, 12*(4), 545–561. https://doi.org/10.1080/19406940.2020.1839532

Wolfe, S. D. (2021). *More than sport: Soft power and potemkinism in the 2018 Men's Football World Cup in Russia* (1st ed.). LIT Verlag. Retrieved September 16, 2021, from https://www.lit-verlag.de/isbn/978-3-643-80370-2

Wolfe, S. D. (2023). The juggernaut endures: Protest, Potemkinism, and Olympic reform. *Leisure Studies, 0*(0), 1–15. https://doi.org/10.1080/02614367.2023.2195201

Wolfe, S. D. (2025). The Quarry Outside My Window: Geographies of Protest in Sochi 2014. In R. Field (Ed.), *Winters of Discontent: The Winter Olympics and a Half Century of Protest and Resistance*, First Edition. University of Illinois Press. https://www.press.uillinois.edu/books/?id=p088445

Wolfe, S. D., Gogishvili, D., & Müller, M. (2024). Mega-events and triple-baseline (un)sustainability. In H. A. Solberg, R. K. Storm, & K. Swart (Eds.), *Research* (pp. 399–414). Edward Elgar Publishing. https://www.e-elgar.com/shop/usd/research-handbook-on-major-sporting-events-9781800885646.html

Open Access This chapter is licensed under the terms of the Creative Commons Attribution 4.0 International License (http://creativecommons.org/licenses/by/4.0/), which permits use, sharing, adaptation, distribution and reproduction in any medium or format, as long as you give appropriate credit to the original author(s) and the source, provide a link to the Creative Commons license and indicate if changes were made.

The images or other third party material in this chapter are included in the chapter's Creative Commons license, unless indicated otherwise in a credit line to the material. If material is not included in the chapter's Creative Commons license and your intended use is not permitted by statutory regulation or exceeds the permitted use, you will need to obtain permission directly from the copyright holder.

CHAPTER 2

Geopolitics and International Sporting Events in the UK: Constitutional Navel-Gazing and the Politics of Event Hosting

Stuart Whigham

Abstract This chapter explores the interconnection between sports event hosting and political symbolism in the UK during a decade of constitutional and political turmoil. It examines the dualistic symbolism of international sporting events such as the Olympics and Commonwealth Games, and the use of sport as a means for political positioning for the UK and its constituent "home nations" of England, Scotland, Wales, and Northern Ireland. Particular focus is given to the UK's attempted use of sporting event hosting for "economic boosterism" and the projection of "soft power," while questioning the effectiveness of this approach in the face of the UK's constitutional turmoil and declining geopolitical influence in the post-Brexit time period.

S. Whigham (✉)
Oxford Brookes University, Oxford, UK
e-mail: swhigham@brookes.ac.uk

© The Author(s) 2025
S. D. Wolfe (ed.), *The Hard Edge of Soft Power*, Mega Event Planning, https://doi.org/10.1007/978-981-96-3515-3_2

Keywords Soft power • Potemkinism • Geopolitics • UK • Olympics • Commonwealth Games

INTRODUCTION

The UK has faced a decade of constitutional and political turmoil, evidenced by the 2014 referendum on Scottish independence, the 2016 referendum on the UK's membership of the European Union, and the subsequent protracted negotiations following the vote for "Brexit" in the 2016 referendum. During this period of constitutional navel-gazing, the UK has hosted (or co-hosted) a number of major international sporting events, including the London 2012 Olympic Games, the Glasgow 2014 Commonwealth Games, the men's 2020 UEFA European Football Championship,[1] the women's 2022 UEFA European Football Championship, and the Birmingham 2022 Commonwealth Games.

This chapter therefore explores the interconnection between sports event hosting and political symbolism in the UK during this period of constitutional navel-gazing, examining the dualistic symbolism of international sporting events such as the Olympics and Commonwealth Games, and the use of sport as a means for political positioning for the UK and its constituent "home nations" of England, Scotland, Wales, and Northern Ireland. Particular emphasis will be placed on the hosting of sporting events in Scotland and England, given that the aforementioned events were hosted primarily in those two nations.

Specific consideration is given to the relative success of these events in achieving the geopolitical aims of the UK during a tumultuous era for politics in Britain, with discussion focusing on: (a) the neoliberal orthodoxy of their associated hosting strategies; (b) the Potemkin nature of the British government's attempts to portray images of British national and constitutional unity; and (c) the fallacy of one of the UK's post-Brexit soft power and economic trade strategies, dubbed "Empire 2.0."

---

[1] The UK hosted 12 matches of the 2020 UEFA European Football Championship as a co-host as part of its multi-nation hosting format, with 8 matches held in London and 4 matches held in Glasgow.

The Politicization of Sports Event Hosting in the UK: An Orthodoxy of Economic Boosterism and Soft Power Projection

Despite a prevalent tendency with the British political sphere to perpetuate the spurious mantra that "sport and politics should not mix," it does not take long to debunk this "myth of autonomy" for sport within the political context of the UK. Although it is fair to say that sport is a relatively marginal issue within the broader political and ideological debates at Westminster and the devolved Parliaments and Assemblies of its constituent nations, sporting issues remain both political and politicized on a regular basis—and this is indeed particularly evident when considering the political import of hosting major international sporting events in the UK.

Given that the hosting of such events requires the investment of vast sums of money from the public exchequer—and, in turn, the maintenance of public support for such investments—it is incumbent on governments to ensure a tangible return from the hosting of international sporting events. In the UK context, this is achieved through the perpetuation of narratives regarding the economic and sporting benefits for the host city and the nation at large, as evident in the discourses surrounding the hosting of events such as the London 2012 Olympic Games, the Glasgow 2014 Commonwealth Games, the men's 2020 UEFA European Football Championship, the women's 2022 UEFA European Football Championship, and the Birmingham 2022 Commonwealth Games. These events were all billed as opportunities to attract visitors to their host cities and regions, thus boosting the regional and national economy through enhanced tourist expenditure and the attraction of inward investment. Furthermore, as epitomized in the "Inspire a Generation" slogan of the London 2012 Olympics, the potential for inspiring participation in sport and physical activity through the promotion of elite sporting role models has remained a central mantra.

It can therefore be argued that the sporting events hosting policy and strategy within the UK and its constituent nations is underpinned by a neoliberal political orthodoxy which frames the benefits of sporting events through the lens of economic boosterism and the projection of soft power (Nye, 1990, 2005) for the UK as a host nation. Indeed, given that the various major events hosted by the UK have been bid for and delivered by governments from across the political spectrum, it is fair to say there has been little challenge to the prevailing political perceptions on the status of sport in the UK context, with little diversity in the ideological approaches to the politics of sport. For example, bidding for the London 2012 Olympics was the brainchild of the "New Labour" government led by Tony Blair and Gordon Brown—but there was little in the way of change in terms of the approach to the event when responsibility of its delivery was assumed by the Conservative/Liberal Democrat coalition government following the 2010 general election. Similarly, the 2014 Glasgow Commonwealth Games, delivered under the Scottish Government led by the pro-independence Scottish National Party, adopted a broadly similar strategic vision of the economic and international reputational benefits of the event for Scotland, albeit with a specific emphasis on the Scottish rather than British context.

Nonetheless, despite this prevailing orthodoxy in the overarching ideological strategies which underpin the hosting of the various sporting events hosted by the UK over the past decade or so, it is important to note that the specific soft power or reputational benefits of each event is shaped by the political considerations at that moment in time. For example, it has been argued that the hosting of the London 2012 Olympics was evidence of the UK attempting to leverage the event to re-brand London and the UK on the global stage during a period of relative decline in terms of geopolitical and economic influence (Grix & Houlihan, 2014; Kenyon et al., 2018). Furthermore, given the threats to the UK's constitutional status from the Scottish independence movement, and the 2014 referendum on Scottish independence which followed from the hosting of the 2012 Olympics and the 2014 Glasgow Commonwealth Games, both events became embroiled within broader political debates regarding the dualistic symbolism of the events in relation to both British and Scottish national identity (Thomas & Antony, 2015; Whigham & Black, 2018). More recent events, such as the hosting of numerous matches of the men's 2020 UEFA Euros and the entire women's 2022 UEFA Euros, were framed as opportunities for post-pandemic economic and socio-cultural recovery. Similarly, the 2022 Birmingham Commonwealth Games were envisaged as an opportunity for the UK to strengthen economic and diplomatic relationships with Commonwealth nations as part of the UK's post-Brexit international trade strategy following its withdrawal from the European Union (de Ruyter et al., 2021).

It is therefore imperative to examine the ways in which it has been possible to maintain a strong degree of ideological consensus in terms of the political goals of hosting these different sporting events within shifting temporal circumstances as various constitutional debates have raged within the UK—and despite the fact that the organizational oversight of these events has varied in terms of complete or shared responsibilities between UK-wide government (e.g. Westminster Parliament), devolved government (e.g. the Scottish Parliament), and local/regional governance (e.g. London Assembly; Greater London Authority; Glasgow City Council; Birmingham City Council; West Midlands Combined Authority). Attention now turns to the processes through which consent for supporting the hosting of events with such ideological fidelity is manufactured within the context of a British constitutional democracy—or, perhaps more aptly, a British "con"-stitutional democracy which highlights the fallacy (hence, "con") of portraying Britain as a fully functioning democratic state.

Manufacturing Consent in a "Con"-stitutional Democracy

In order to understand the complexity of the linkages of *external* geopolitics and the hosting of international sporting events by the UK, it is imperative to contextualize the complexities of the *internal* constitutional relationships and political dynamics within the UK. The characterization of the UK as a "con"-stitutional democracy is a useful tool for contextualizing the dysfunctional and asymmetric constitutional arrangements evident within the UK "state," given the contrasting degrees of political autonomy and legislative powers granted the devolved Parliaments (i.e. Scotland) and Assemblies (i.e. Wales; Northern Ireland) of its constituent "nations" vis-à-vis those powers "reserved" by the UK state for the UK-wide Parliament at Westminster. Given that each of these devolved legislative bodies has contrasting degrees of power within the UK's constitutional arrangements, it is unsurprising that "nationalist" political parties who are in favour of greater devolved powers—and their electoral supporters in the general public—frequently highlighted the lack of democratic power for the devolved nations in a situation where the UK Government retains an effective "veto" through its retention of "reserved powers" on key policy areas.

Turning attention to the Scottish context, the 1997 Scotland Bill legislated for a referendum on the re-establishment of a devolved Scottish Parliament in 1999 with legislative powers over all areas except for "reserved powers" which would remain under the Westminster Parliament. These "reserved powers" were macro-economic policy, foreign policy, defence, social security, abortion, broadcasting, immigration, and border controls (Devine, 1999). Following the re-establishment of the Scottish Parliament in 1999, Scottish politicians have therefore had the opportunity to pursue distinct strategies to promote certain Scottish economic, social, and political goals using "devolved powers." It is important to note that sport policy was identified as a policy domain which could be devolved to the various national Parliaments and Assemblies. One such strategy has seen Scotland, and particularly Glasgow, actively pursue a range of sporting events as part of an economic development strategy underpinned by tourism promotion, infrastructural improvements, and urban regeneration (Chaney, 2015; Matheson, 2010).

While the establishment of the Scottish Parliament was originally envisaged by the UK-wide Labour-led Westminster Government as a solution to quell the arguments of pro-independence parties such as the Scottish National Party (SNP), the SNP continued to gain traction with the electorate through its decision to embrace devolution as part of a long-term gradualist strategy towards Scottish independence:

> The party's leader Alex Salmond … argued that it made better sense to work within the parliament, and to ensure it delivered policies which would benefit the new Scotland. Then, when Scots voters realized what it had managed to achieve, the SNP would be able to claim that, with independence, even more might be gained. (Linklater, 2000, p. 227)

Although the constitutional arrangements limited the ability of the SNP administration to implement its manifesto policies, including a proposed independence referendum, the formation of the first SNP minority government in the Scottish Parliament in 2007 offered the party the opportunity to demonstrate its ability to govern competently, simultaneously providing a forum for emphasizing the benefits of Scottish independence (Cairney, 2011; Dardanelli & Mitchell, 2014; Johns et al., 2013).

At the subsequent 2011 elections, the SNP was able to exploit dissatisfaction with the Labour government following the global financial crisis of 2007–2008, and the return of the Scottish "democratic deficit" at Westminster with the establishment of the coalition between the Conservatives and the Liberal Democrats following the 2010 general election (Mycock, 2012). The result of the 2011 Scottish Parliament elections placed the SNP in a position to hold an independence referendum, with its 69 MSPs providing the party with an overall majority. The SNP-led Scottish government entered into negotiations with the coalition Westminster government, resulting in the signing of the "Edinburgh Agreement" in October 2012 which legislated for a single-question referendum before the end of 2014, in line with the SNP's preference for a referendum date in autumn 2014.

The Potemkin Façade of Constitutional Unity at London 2012 and Glasgow 2014

The 2014 Scottish independence referendum saw 55.3% of the electorate voting "No" to Scottish independence as opposed to 44.7% voting "Yes," to the disappointment of the pro-independence "Yes" campaign led primarily by the SNP and the Scottish Greens. Nonetheless, the "con"-stitutional nature of British democracy was subsequently brought back to the fore by advocates of Scottish independence due to the outcome of the 2016 UK-wide referendum on European Union (EU) membership which resulted in a victory for the anti-EU "Leave" campaign which supported the UK's withdrawal from the EU—or "Brexit" as has now become common parlance—despite strong electoral support in Scotland to "Remain" within the EU (McEwen, 2018). Political nationalism and electoral support for the prospect of Scotland's secession from the UK has thus remained high in recent years. Similar constitutional challenges have been created by Brexit in Northern Ireland and Wales—particularly so in the former context of Northern Ireland, given the complex challenges of agreeing a satisfactory arrangement between the UK and the EU with regards to customs and border arrangements on the island of Ireland between the EU state of the Republic of Ireland and the UK territory in Northern Ireland.

Given that the UK government continues to grapple with the contrasting and competing forces of British, English, Scottish, Welsh, Northern Irish, and Irish nationalism during a period of constitutional instability, one might assume that any investigation of the impact of the complex internal politics of hosting international sporting events within the UK's current "con"-stitutional democracy would identify stark contrasts between the respective governments in their ideological and strategic approach to event hosting. However, in the case of approaches adopted by the various political actors responsible for the bidding, organization, and delivery processes for major international sporting events, a strong degree of ideological orthodoxy with regards to hosting strategies has remained evident regardless of this constitutional turmoil. As discussed at the outset, the overarching strategies for these events framed their benefits through the lens of economic boosterism and the projection of soft power for the UK as a host nation, evidencing a neoliberal political orthodoxy maintained by political parties and governments with contrasting views on the UK's constitutional arrangements.

Nonetheless, turning away from the hosting strategies of the events to focus upon the political framing and symbolism of the events does shed some light on the impact of the UK's complex constitutional arrangements. For example, the London 2012 Olympic Games took place during a period where Scotland's status within the UK was high on the political agenda in the summer preceding the aforementioned Edinburgh Agreement of October 2012 which facilitated the 2014 Scottish independence referendum. London 2012 thus became an opportunity for the UK government to emphasize the united nature of Team GB in both the context of sport and geopolitics more broadly, given that the Olympics is organized with representative teams from nation-states and necessitates an integrated Great Britain representative team—rather than the separate English, Scottish, Welsh, and Northern Irish teams evident in other international sporting events in football, rugby, and hockey (among others), or events such as the Commonwealth Games. As Boyle and Haynes (2014) argued, the Games "revealed a temporary suspension in the pressing debate on Scottish independence, with hegemonic Britishness and the symbolic flying of the Union Jack more in evidence across the UK than had been witnessed in recent decades" (p. 91), with the well-received London 2012 Olympic Ceremony directed by Danny Boyle presented as a case in point.

However, the façade of constitutional unity has been strongly undermined by subsequent events which have plagued political and constitutional debates with the UK, thus evidencing the arguments woven throughout this collection regarding the existence of Potemkinism in the UK government's attempts to foster and portray a shared British identity through London 2012 and sporting events more generally.

Firstly, the 2014 Glasgow Commonwealth Games were hosted in closer proximity to the Scottish independence referendum, and were thus more closely intertwined with the constitutional debate. The 2014 Games afforded an opportunity for pro-independence campaigners to draw upon the symbolism of the event with its separate representative teams for the home nations to underpin their own political positions. For the SNP, the successful organization of the Games acted as an illustration of Scotland's capacity for political self-governance, while simultaneously framing the lack of full control over the economic benefits of the event as an illustration of broader discontentment with the constitutional status quo and the "democratic deficit" of Scotland's status within the Union.

In contrast, pro-union parties such as Labour and the Conservatives framed the Games and the constitutional status quo as the "best of both worlds," highlighting the economic and logistical support from the UK Government for the Games, as well as the mutually co-existing expressions of Britishness and Scottishness.

Although the dualistic nature of the symbolism of London 2012 and Glasgow 2014 arguably rendered any politicization of the events as a zero-sum game offering neither side a specific opportunity to gain a political advantage, this overt political struggle in terms of the framing of the 2014 Games demonstrates that any claims of fostering constitutional unity through hosting sporting events in the UK remain a Potemkin fallacy.

"Empire 2.0": The UK's Fading Post-Brexit Soft Power

More recent international sporting events hosted in the UK—such as numerous matches of the men's 2020 UEFA Euros, the entire women's 2022 UEFA Euros, and the 2022 Birmingham Commonwealth Games—also possess analytical import for understanding the geopolitical context for the UK's sporting event hosting strategy. For example, in a tumultuous economic period for the UK due to the impact of Brexit and the 2020 COVID-19 pandemic, these events became framed as opportunities for post-pandemic economic and socio-cultural recovery, and envisaged as an opportunity for the UK to strengthen economic and diplomatic relationships with Commonwealth nations as part of the UK's post-Brexit international trade strategy following its withdrawal from the EU (de Ruyter et al., 2021; Whigham & Black, 2018).

This proposed geopolitical pivot by the UK government from the EU to the Commonwealth was labelled by some commentators as the launch of an "Empire 2.0" strategy, which envisaged a replacement of the strong economic and diplomatic relationships with the EU—lost due to Brexit—with alternative trade deals with Commonwealth nations who have existing political and diplomatic links with the UK, albeit on a more geographically dispersed basis than the EU's trading arrangements (Adler-Nissen et al., 2017; Honeyman, 2023; Langan, 2023; Olusoga, 2017). Indeed, Boris Johnson, the former prime minister and prominent anti-EU "Leave" campaigner, suggested that

> [a]s we re-examine our relationship with the European Union, we have a vital opportunity to recast our immigration system in just this way. And the first place to start is with the Commonwealth. (quoted in Mason, 2014)

Given that the UK's relationships with its Commonwealth nations dwindled since the establishment of the European Economic Community in 1951, such a strategy was viewed as presenting an opportunity to redress the decline of the intra-Commonwealth economic and political community following a period where the Commonwealth's utility as an effective global force was diminished by the Cold War, the geopolitical dominance of the USA, and the UK's embrace of pan-European co-operation. However, the potential to leverage the UK's hosting vis-à-vis this new "Empire 2.0" soft power strategy was significantly undermined by both foreseeable and unforeseeable factors.

Firstly, the attempts to replace existing economic and diplomatic relationships with the EU with alternative trade deals with Commonwealth nations have proved predictably challenging. An obvious factor hampering any such attempts to replace trading links lost through Brexit is the complexity and extended timescales in ratifying individual trade deals with dozens of different independent nation-states within the Commonwealth—a much more complex process than dealing with an established trading bloc such as the EU. Furthermore, where trading deals have been struck between the UK and non-EU nations, they have often been on a much smaller scale in terms of their potential benefits for gross domestic product for the UK economy given the smaller size of the economies of non-EU states in comparison to the EU bloc (Du et al., 2023; Garcia, 2023). Finally—and perhaps most importantly in terms of geopolitical and diplomatic considerations—the UK's sudden embrace of the Commonwealth has understandably been met by cynicism by a number of Commonwealth nations given the legacy of Empire and the lack of self-reflection from UK political actors on the asymmetric, dysfunctional, and hierarchical nature of the post-colonial Commonwealth system (Honeyman, 2023; Langan, 2023). Therefore, any attempts to establish an "Empire 2.0", which places Commonwealth nations on equal footing within future political and economic relations, require significant efforts from the UK to redress the perpetuation of whitewashed representations of the UK's imperial legacy—and the hosting of international sporting events will do little in the way of achieving this, regardless of their potential symbolism for the UK's relationship with Commonwealth nations.

Secondly, the devastating impact of the COVID-19 pandemic on global societies and economies unsurprisingly had significant consequences for the delivery of international sporting events, including those scheduled to be hosted in the UK (Poulaki et al., 2023; Ricordel et al., 2023). Given that the pandemic resulted in travel restrictions and social distancing measures, international sporting events were postponed with reduced attendance capacities and international visitors or held in line with their planned schedules but again with reduced capacities. This meant that the achievement of the planned "legacies" of these events—whether economic, sporting, socio-cultural, or geopolitical—was rendered highly unlikely (Ricordel et al., 2023), given that legacy claims have often been proven to be futile even in normal conditions prior to COVID-19. For the UK, this meant that any attempts to leverage these three major international sporting events for long-term geopolitical, diplomatic, and economic strategic goals in a post-Brexit era were significantly thwarted.

Given the impact of these developments on the UK's plans for international sporting events, it can be argued that the recent strategic approach to event hosting has failed to achieve many of the originally envisaged economic and geopolitical goals. Indeed, with regards to the Commonwealth Games' long-held status as a symbol of inter-Commonwealth diplomatic ties, this strategy could be further undermined by the challenges in finding a host for the 2026 Commonwealth Games following the withdrawal of the Australian state of Victoria as the proposed host in the summer of 2023 (Ingle, 2023; Ricordel et al., 2023). At the time of writing, it remains to be seen whether the short-notice agreement for Glasgow to step into the breach to host the 2026 Games will be sufficient to demonstrate the ongoing viability of the Commonwealth Games, or whether this will simply prove to be the last iteration of the event in a worse-case, yet possible, scenario—perhaps a fitting analogy for the UK's fading soft power and the failure of its flawed "Empire 2.0" geopolitical strategy.

Conclusion

The UK's ability to harness recent international sporting events to achieve its broader geopolitical aims has been, at best, highly questionable. Firstly, the sustained ideological alignment of the various host governments—both UK-wide and within the devolved nations—with a neoliberal orthodoxy vis-à-vis the hosting of international events has left the host nations prone to the same challenges of delivering meaningful, long-term economic, social, and political benefits as all other hosts of major international sporting events. This emphasis on economic motives has left the UK's event hosting strategy prone to broader economic downturns, as witnessed through the impact of Brexit, the COVID-19 pandemic, and the outbreak of conflict between Russia and Ukraine.

Furthermore, the politically naïve attempts to portray a Potemkin façade of constitutional unity within the UK and diplomatic warmth between the UK and other Commonwealth nations have undermined its ability to foster a sustainable soft power strategy as part of its geopolitical relations in the post-Brexit era, with the symbolism of these sporting events illustrating the fallacy of this strategic approach. Nonetheless, the UK has continued to bid for hosting rights for future events, winning the right to host the UEFA 2028 Men's European Football Championship across the UK and the Republic of Ireland, in part with a view to projecting an image of co-operation between these nations in the post-Brexit era. Thus, as governments of developed economies across the globe begin to illustrate a greater degree of scepticism about the wisdom of hosting international sporting events, it can be concluded that the UK's recent experiences can and should be held as a "case in point" about the potential risks of such strategic approaches to the use of sporting events to achieve geopolitical goals, and the challenges the UK will face in fully achieving its strategic aims for events such as Euro 2028 (and beyond).

References

Adler-Nissen, R., Galpin, C., & Rosamond, B. (2017). Performing Brexit: How a post-Brexit world is imagined outside the United Kingdom. *The British Journal of Politics and International Relations, 19*(3), 573–591. https://doi.org/10.1177/1369148117711092

Boyle, R., & Haynes, R. (2014). Watching the games. In V. Girginov (Ed.), *Handbook of the London 2012 Olympic and Paralympic Games—Volume 2: Celebrating the games* (pp. 84–95). Routledge.

Cairney, P. (2011). Coalition and minority government in Scotland: Lessons for the United Kingdom? *The Political Quarterly*, *82*(2), 261–269. https://doi.org/10.1111/j.1467-923X.2011.02184.x

Chaney, P. (2015). Electoral discourse and the party politicization of sport in multi-level systems: Analysis of UK elections 1945–2011. *International Journal of Sport Policy and Politics*, *7*(2), 159–180. https://doi.org/10.1080/19406940.2014.921230

Dardanelli, P., & Mitchell, J. (2014). An independent Scotland? The Scottish National Party's bid for independence and its prospects. *The International Spectator*, *49*(3), 88–105. https://doi.org/10.1080/03932729.2014.935996

de Ruyter, A., Hearne, D., Beer, J., & Zaman, Y. (2021). Brexit, Birmingham and the 2022 Commonwealth Games: An opportunity for regeneration and rejuvenation? *Managing Sport and Leisure*, *26*(5), 413–428. https://doi.org/10.1080/23750472.2020.1820369

Devine, T. M. (1999). *The Scottish nation: 1700–2000*. Penguin.

Du, J., Satoglu, E., & Shepotylo, O. (2023). How did Brexit affect UK trade? *Contemporary Social Science*, *18*(2), 266–283. https://doi.org/10.1080/21582041.2023.2192043

Garcia, M. (2023). Post-Brexit trade policy in the UK: Placebo policy-making? *Journal of European Public Policy*, *30*(11), 2492–2518. https://doi.org/10.1080/13501763.2023.2235380

Grix, J., & Houlihan, B. (2014). Sports mega-events as part of a nation's soft power strategy: The cases of Germany (2006) and the UK (2012). *The British Journal of Politics and International Relations*, *16*(4), 572–596. https://doi.org/10.1111/1467-856X.12017

Honeyman, V. (2023). The Johnson factor: British national identity and Boris Johnson. *British Politics*, *18*(1), 40–59. https://doi.org/10.1057/s41293-022-00211-0

Ingle, S. (2023, December 4). No UK rescue for 2026 Commonwealth Games after Gold Coast withdrawal. *The Guardian*. Retrieved January 23, 2024, from https://www.theguardian.com/sport/2023/dec/04/commonwealth-games-in-turmoil-as-gold-coast-drops-bid-to-host-in-2026

Johns, R., Mitchell, J., & Carman, C. (2013). Constitution or competence? The SNP's re-election in 2011. *Political Studies*, *61*(S1), 158–178. https://doi.org/10.1111/1467-9248.12016

Kenyon, J., Manoli, A., & Bodet, G. (2018). Brand consistency and coherency at the London 2012 Olympic Games. *Journal of Strategic Marketing*, *26*(1), 6–18. https://doi.org/10.1080/0965254X.2017.1293139

Langan, M. (2023). *Global Britain and neo-colonialism in Africa: Brexit, 'development' and coloniality*. Palgrave Macmillan. https://doi.org/10.1007/978-3-031-42482-3

Linklater, M. (2000). The settled will of the Scottish people. In F. Maclean (Ed.), *Scotland: A concise history* (pp. 224–231). Thames and Hudson.

Mason, R. (2014, November 3). Osborne downplays row with Germany over EU freedom of movement. *The Guardian*. Retrieved January 23, 2024, from https://www.theguardian.com/world/2014/nov/03/george-osborne-downplays-difference-germany-eu-freedom-movement

Matheson, C. (2010). Legacy planning, regeneration and events: The Glasgow 2014 Commonwealth Games. *Local Economy, 25*(1), 10–23. https://doi.org/10.1080/02690940903545364

McEwen, N. (2018). Brexit and Scotland: Between two unions. *British Politics, 13*(1), 65–78. https://doi.org/10.1057/s41293-017-0066-4

Mycock, A. (2012). SNP, identity and citizenship: Re-imagining state and nation. *National Identities, 14*(1), 53–69. https://doi.org/10.1080/14608944.2012.657078

Nye, J. (1990). Soft power. *Foreign Policy, 80*, 153–171. https://doi.org/10.2307/1148580

Nye, J. (2005). *Soft power: The means to success in world politics*. Public Affairs.

Olusoga, D. (2017, March 19). Empire 2.0 is dangerous nostalgia for something that never existed. *The Guardian*. Retrieved January 24, 2024, from https://www.theguardian.com/commentisfree/2017/mar/19/empire-20-is-dangerous-nostalgia-for-something-that-never-existed

Poulaki, P., Kritikos, A., Vasilakis, N., & Valeri, M. (2023). Sports tourism in the COVID-19 era. In M. Valeri (Ed.), *Sport and tourism* (pp. 41–53). Emerald.

Ricordel, P., Whittam, G., & Wise, N. (2023). Editorial: Sports, politics and legacy: Building back better? *Local Economy, 38*(4), 303–305. https://doi.org/10.1177/02690942231213592

Thomas, R., & Antony, M. (2015). Competing constructions of British national identity: British newspaper comment on the 2012 Olympics opening ceremony. *Media, Culture & Society, 37*(3), 493–503. https://doi.org/10.1177/0163443715574671

Whigham, S., & Black, J. (2018). Glasgow 2014, the media and Scottish politics: The (post) imperial symbolism of the Commonwealth Games. *The British Journal of Politics and International Relations, 20*(2), 360–378. https://doi.org/10.1177/1369148117737279

Open Access This chapter is licensed under the terms of the Creative Commons Attribution 4.0 International License (http://creativecommons.org/licenses/by/4.0/), which permits use, sharing, adaptation, distribution and reproduction in any medium or format, as long as you give appropriate credit to the original author(s) and the source, provide a link to the Creative Commons license and indicate if changes were made.

The images or other third party material in this chapter are included in the chapter's Creative Commons license, unless indicated otherwise in a credit line to the material. If material is not included in the chapter's Creative Commons license and your intended use is not permitted by statutory regulation or exceeds the permitted use, you will need to obtain permission directly from the copyright holder.

CHAPTER 3

When the Stage Came Down: A Short-Term Feel-Good Experience at South Africa's World Cup

Rutendo Roselyn Musikavanhu

Abstract This chapter argues that the strategy for realizing soft power through the hosting of mega-events has not been wholly successful. This discussion demonstrates that the act of pursuing soft power and national regeneration can negatively affect the host community's sense of wellbeing. This can result in trade-offs such as the misallocation of community resources as governments prioritize their public diplomacy interests. By outlining the theoretical dimensions of the concept of Potemkinism, the chapter unpacks the characterization and evaluation of how the FIFA 2010 World Cup in South Africa was a short-lived feel-good experience. The World Cup appears to have given governing bodies in South Africa a rationale for the reallocation of funds, thus creating a superficial surface that hid a different reality underneath. The concern raised by the respondents reveals that community members were largely knowledgeable about the potential negative outcomes associated with the excessive use of public funds and resources. However, their voices were overlooked. The findings

R. R. Musikavanhu (✉)
Musikavanhu, University of Westminster, London, UK
e-mail: R.Musikavanhu@westminster.ac.uk

have important implications for examining how nations, in particular emerging countries, are increasingly using mega-events as part of their soft power strategies. Rather than coercion, it could be of value to consider community engagement.

Keywords Soft power • Potemkinism • South Africa • Football World Cup

Overview

This chapter explores discourse relating to the socio-economics and politics of hosting mega-events in emerging territories, looking at the example of South Africa. Developed nations have for many years used mega-events as a soft power tool that has allowed them to enhance their national profiles, garner more tourism, and reinforce their financial and political standing (Andranovich et al., 2001; Nye, 2021). Andranovich et al. (ibid.) explore the relationship between host nations and the desire for public diplomacy through the hosting of mega-events, identifying attempts not only to leverage a legacy that positively showcases the host nation internationally but also to hasten national redevelopment plans while expanding upon territorial presence. According to Murray (2018 in Skey, 2023, p. 756):

> Diplomacy and soft power are both often portrayed as a positive feature of international relations, by focusing on the manner in which states and state institutions look to manage (potential) conflicts and build relationships through engagement and attraction rather than deception.

Perhaps the most serious challenge is the payoff associated with these strategies, and the effects on a nation's reputation alongside the investments made toward improving life for the host community (Grix et al., 2019). Likewise, Nye (2021, p. 201) observes a correlation between "smart strategy … attraction and persuasion." This has also been interpreted as the diplomatic activity of nation (re)branding that helps alter reputations in a way that favors promoting national agendas (Skey, 2023).

Like their developed nation counterparts, several emerging states have been observed to align their national (re)development strategies to the pursuit of mega-events. Inevitably, the goal is to wield the anticipated benefits as a conduit for development and access to the global stage (Grix et al., 2019). Certainly, the advantage of hosting mega-events is seen as an accelerator for catalytic development. However, such expositions are not without their critics. Andranovich et al. (2001, p. 114) explain that mega-events present a vehicle that offers justification for the reallocation of funds—habitually "scarce resources"—and the pursuit of "economic development activities and attention for competitive gain" often at the cost of other more pressing needs. One aspect that illustrates this challenge has been explained as Potemkinism, which Wolfe (2023, p. 3) terms as "a superficial covering (that) can conceal unpleasant realities." Potemkinism offers language to suggest that a relationship exists between the pursuit of mega-events for socio-economic and political gain, and potential host nations going to great lengths striving to put on a show with limited resources. According to Wolfe (ibid. p. 4), this tendency to overplay reality "via the projection of an unproblematic but superficial image" hinders true development. Instead, this overzealous approach to present a superficial image engenders destructive outcomes.

Dowse and Fletcher (2020) question this "silver bullet approach" and the true ability of mega-events to offer a single solution to bridge governmental desires while delivering development that is beneficial to all. The limited involvement of necessary control groups, such as the community, has enabled particular interest groups (e.g., event and national governing bodies) to use mega-events for their personal interests over realizing lasting shared goals (Cornelissen & Maennig, 2010). This inconsistency suggests a degree of imbalance, which enables this chapter to raise questions about the realization of transformative social change as underpinned by political agendas. The purpose of this chapter is to review the first-hand lived experiences of community members from the FIFA 2010 World Cup, South Africa. Through the analysis of their narrative stories, this chapter offers a different understanding of the impact of the socio-economics and politics associated with hosting mega-events in emerging territories.

THE SOUTH AFRICAN EXPERIENCE

Having been banned from the Fèdèration Internationale de Football Association (FIFA) in 1961 and the International Olympic Committee (IOC) ahead of the 1964 Tokyo Olympics, South Africa's emergence from apartheid between 1900 and 1994 marked its re-entry onto the international scene. In 1994, South Africa went through a period of change from the political institution of apartheid to one of majority rule that favors democracy. It also hosted the 1995 Rugby World Cup (Van Der Merwe, 2007). In this post-apartheid era, and in a bid to change perceptions in both international and regional communities, South Africa saw mega-events as a vehicle to help realize social reconciliation, achieve national development, and international acceptance. Although the apartheid era had left South Africa with a tainted image locally and abroad, "tying the idea of nation building to sport began for South Africa when President Mandela attempted to utilize the national pride derived from hosting and winning the 1995 Rugby World Cup to achieve social reconciliation goals" (Gibson, 2014, p. 114).

The 1995 Rugby World Cup was an iconic event that was seen to have helped pave the way for "the Rainbow Nation" and South Africa's quest to develop international relations (Mitchell, 2015). Hosting the 1995 Rugby World Cup remains significant to the nation's development. It marked the beginning of togetherness across the divided communities of South Africa, and this was partly achieved through hosting a mega-event that encouraged engagement and a sense of community. In the lead up to the 2010 FIFA World Cup the National Tourism Ministry took on the slogans "South Africa; It is Possible," and the "Ke Nako! Campaign," a Sotho saying that means "It Is Time," aimed to help celebrate and acknowledge the arrival of South Africa on the international stage (Cornelissen & Maennig, 2010). As such, mega-events presented not only South Africa the chance to foster and realize a sense of national identity and nationalism but also the opportunity to exercise political power and participation on a larger stage.

Poor event management and lack of transparency surrounding the hosting of events in developing nations have resulted in overspending and the displacement of community members (Maharaj, 2015). Notably, those experiences generated problematic long-term impacts that resulted in greater inequalities among the underprivileged who are relatively less privileged than those from developed countries. Arguably, developing nations are beset with more challenging socio-economic, socio-cultural, socio-environmental, and socio-political circumstances as compared to developed nations. This could be a significant impediment to governments pursuing mega-events in those nations. Developing countries tend to have vast social inequalities which can be observed in the great disparities, influencing social divisions, among other social issues (Van Der Merwe, 2007).

Hosting mega-events in communities from developing nations can put undue pressure on communities that already have limited resources (Cornelissen & Maennig, 2010). The outcomes of mega-events could affect those communities in more harmful ways as compared to their developed nation counterparts, including the questionable legacy of burdensome debts absorbed by the host community, impractical infrastructures, and displacement from one's community through gentrification (Rocha et al., 2017).

In the socio-political discourse of mega-event studies, it remains important to explore community experiences of mega-events from the context of developing nations. In particular, it is crucial to see how the persuasive approach to international relations through the social influence of mega-events affects community experiences and perceptions. The results in this chapter are based upon a wider study conducted by Musikavanhu (2019). The reflections are extracted from narrative stories collected from 17 Green Point Community members, a community located in the City of Cape Town which partly hosted the event. Green Point was host to the opening day, quarter, and semi-final soccer games of the 2010 FIFA World Cup. These individuals were Green Point residents and had constant interaction with the World Cup. Through a review of primary data collected on the 2010 FIFA World Cup six years after the event, this chapter also seeks to understand whether soft power and international showcasing leads to accelerated social development. Additionally, exploring whether staging mega-events provides emerging powers with opportunities to generate attention that truly engenders togetherness evokes the "feel-good" factor among its citizens, and whether this has knock-on effects on their quality of life and sense of wellbeing. The stories shared helped to "capture the richness and nuances of meaning in human affairs" (Polkinghorne, 1995, p. 11).

When the Stage Came Down

Community members from Green Point felt somewhat let down by promises that did not materialize or last long beyond the experience of the event. A number of those promises of a better quality of life were informed by the political propaganda around leveraging a legacy of national development. However, through the respondents' stories it appears that prioritizing South Africa's international (re)branding came at the cost of guaranteeing long-lasting social development for all. One of the issues that emerge from these findings relates to the idea of how life changed after the stage came down.

> Post the World Cup, because the euphoria kind of died down, we began to see the impacts and implications of having the World Cup. The reason why I said after, is I went to watch another football match at the Athlone stadium and Athlone as a neighborhood is not as developed as Green Point, it's not as accessible or as safe as Green Point, so all of these experiences that I had watching the World Cup and things were much easier to access and it was safer. Coming out of the World Cup and attending a game at Athlone made me realize that oh, this is the actual reality of hosting a football match in South Africa. At that point it felt as the euphoria was almost staged for the world to see. After all was said and done the euphoria came to an end and the stage came down. (Tilda)[1]

It can be seen through Tilda's extract how this event had been hosted to attract international attention to position South Africa in a particular light (see Cornelissen & Maennig, 2010; Mitchell, 2015; Skey, 2023). In agreement, Florence also indicates the experience felt like a bubble.

> In preparation for the World Cup there was a lot of improvement to the infrastructure—new buildings, new hotels, and other hotels were renovated to take care of the tourists that were going to come to this country to watch the matches. Um, even business in general improved a lot. ... However, the local people in Green Point, mmmh somehow some were not happy, some of the people that stayed closer to the venue were moved away, and you could see that they were not happy. (Florence)

After the bubble had burst it seems that the imperfections began to creep in, and this was not perceivable during the World Cup (see Wolfe, 2023). The emergence of those experiences appears to have resulted in a sense of disgruntlement, as expressed by Brenda:

> Now, with the economic hardships going on, it's like ah some people are not happy anymore especially the locals. They feel that the foreigners are now exceeding them and are taking their opportunities so that happiness is somehow slowly dying away. (Brenda)

---

[1] All names have been changed in order to safeguard anonymity.

Below, Florence articulates changes that occurred in preparation for the World Cup, including the displacement of community members. It appears the host location of Green Point was "hiding" people as a way to disassociate Green Point with the image of poverty and to gain a new identity.

> Some of the few shops were moved away in Green Point; they removed some shops and raised big new hotels to take care of the tourists. Some of the houses that were not looking nice were removed and the people were moved away, even the street people, you know these guys who stay on the streets, during the World Cup can you believe it, they were all taken away and put far away in a place somewhere fenced, so they don't distract the World Cup happenings. The beggars were taken off the streets because you know, they would be distracting the people. ... I was not very happy about what happened to those people but what can you do?" (Florence)

Florence's depiction of events gives life to the conceptualization of the Potemkin spectacle. It can be seen that the event was "a superficial covering [that] concealed unpleasant realities" (Wolfe, 2023, p. 3). Looking at Karoline's experience, this new identity came with the price tag of an unsustainable lifestyle, increased community discontentment, and a sense of conflict over the event's true impact.

> In terms of property and gentrification, what we did is we just scaled down; we sold our Bed and Breakfast hotel, after the hotel became too big and the rates kept going up. So, we just scaled right down and also moved to a much smaller home, our rates have gone up and there are people in family homes and other people that may be renting and can no longer afford. I don't know if it's fair, I don't think it's fair, but the area has changed and circumstances have changed. ... Green Point is growing, Cape Town is growing, it's one of the fastest growing cities in the world. I feel that we have to come to terms with that or just move to the country. (Karoline)

The event had been presented as an opportunity for social development with benefits for all (Grix et al., 2019). Instead, the vulnerable and marginalized members of this community were overlooked, and the opportunity did not positively impact their livelihoods.

> During the event, there was not even one beggar, I felt so bad because those people wanted to benefit from the tourists, but where they were put, I hear they were given food and so on, but they were not used to being locked

inside a fence, so I felt bad. But in another way maybe it was a good thing so we could give a good impression to the visitors? I felt bad but it was to the advantage of the city [sighs]. I still feel bad even after all these years, I can see that they lacked an opportunity to benefit, they still need some help, and they are accumulating in numbers now. (Florence)

Jackson's story tells how the city officials' decision to host the event in picturesque Green Point prioritized official interests while overlooking the needs of the community. The approach suggests the planning of the event was not particularly inclusive as they were acting in a way that appeared to not be representative of the community's interests.

So initially the community was very against the event altogether, and in fact there was a big community movement and demonstration against having it here in Green Point—not against having the World Cup, but against having it on the Green Point Common. In fact, we understand that a lot of law was sidelined and bypassed in order to get the event here. It was actually quite illegal what was done. We [Community Ratepayers Association] eventually had a big meeting with the mayor, and she appealed to us to support the event. ... So, there was a lot of anger, and a lot of suspicion and frustration and concern about the expense ... the officials essentially sidelined us, we spent a lot of time planning, but they basically put us to the side and ignored a lot of what we said. We did achieve some things, in terms of specifically planting the trees along the roads. (Jackson)

Jane appears frustrated by how the community now seems to have inherited infrastructure that has failed to generate a sense of longevity (see Rocha et al., 2017). Instead, they are now saddled by some expensive underutilized infrastructure.

To be honest I didn't really think about whether we could really afford the event. People look at South Africa as the most modern country in Africa, so that wasn't really my concern. Afterwards I was disappointed as we have all these beautiful stadiums and I feel like something should have been done with them but instead they are just withering away and that feels like a bit of a waste of my tax money. (Jane)

This concern is echoed by Jackson, who highlights the community's concerns leading up to the event and how the council was spending the public's money on the event. Those concerns appear to align with Jane's reflections from after the event that confirm there was a seemingly poorly thought-out longer-term plan.

> Our concerns were mainly two things; the first thing was the expense the city would have to incur in everything that would have to be built—the stadium etc. and whether the city could afford it in light of its other priorities and in light of the fact that we are a city with poor people and few ratepayers, and there's a great need to spend our money very carefully. (Jackson)

Through Jackson's reflection it is clear to see that the residents were knowledgeable about the negative experiences taking place in their community. However, the concern appears to be that their voices do not matter as they were not being listened to. Tilda also questions the underutilized stadium and the distribution of community resources that she appears to feel were misallocated in preparation for the event (see Andranovich et al., 2001).

> So it started to make me think about and dig into the experiences that the other locals had and why did we have to build a stadium that was going to be a sitting duck when we could have refurbished Athlone stadium. A lot of the locals could have benefited from better roads, better infrastructure, access to My-Citi the bus route, access to better transport systems. Had the WC been at Athlone stadium, instead that was invested in upmarket Green Point instead. Why should that community of Athlone have to suffer at the expense of the community in Green Point that is already well off? (Tilda)

Tessa gives substantial background information that in part offers an explanation for the nation's desire to invest in the image of South Africa during this time and how this reimaging could influence international perceptions (see Gibson, 2014).

> There were definitely some concerns and wondering how the world is actually going to receive us, and we were also wondering how eager people would actually be to come down to Africa. ... Um I would say, afterwards, now, the question becomes so what shall we do with all of this stuff? Because most certainly there was a very grand financial investment placed so we would be able to host it. The hosting was magnificent, it was well executed, it was brilliant, however even with that being said, we are still sitting with a whole lot of infrastructure that is being underutilized and so particularly Green Point Stadium. There's a friend of mine who's actually doing a study

in particular about soccer matches, the soccer matches that are played in Green Point and Athlone, and it turns out that the fans, more of them are situated in Athlone and so more of the fans actually go and watch soccer only when its being played in Athlone, and Green Point which hosts 60,000—I think is the seating. Usually, the capacity reaches about 4,000, that's round about the maximum that they can reach and so the actual capacity of these places isn't being reached. (Tessa)

Tessa also explains the existence of another stadium in a less desirable part of Cape Town—a part of Cape Town where soccer already had a stronghold prior to the World Cup. This makes Tessa question why the Council saw fit to overlook this stadium in favor of building a new stadium that would most likely wind up underutilized for a number of the reasons she articulates. Karoline also reflects upon the location of stadium and shares some insight into how Green Point possibly became the location of the event.

Rumor has it, I don't know how true it is, that Sepp Blatter [FIFA President] was in a helicopter, and he flew over Green Point and he saw Table Mountain and said this is where I want it to be, and it was kind of like the deal breaker and that is what had to happen. So and as you probably know already, the residents fought tooth and nail, and the other big issue is that it was public land, it was never actually the state's land, it was public land and the original amount of land that was granted to the public for use has shrunk over the years as the city council or whichever governing body responsible at the time has essentially appropriated that land for their own use. So lucky for us we did have some residents who fought and they accepted that the stadium was going to go ahead, and they managed to get some trade-offs, and we do have a lovely park. (Karoline)

Karoline's reflection on the issue of community ownership shows how the people of Green Point fought to protect their community. However, they ultimately experienced a sense of diminishing power as the city council's authority increased. This frustration on the expenditure of the taxpayer's money is echoed by Andrew. He suggests perhaps the community ought to respond in rebellion and that way they can be taken more seriously by the council.

What I have suggested a few times is that we need to have a broad-based tax revolt and say here's a list of things the city should be looking after, and it's not being taken care of, so at the particular date we will not pay taxes until you take care of these things. The current Mayor is a weak individual and doesn't have the standards to say no, people have to do their jobs, etc. (Andrew)

Turning to how inclusive the experience was, Jessica feels that certain people in society were able to participate while others were marginalized due to affordability. This is a polarizing outcome, more so considering how the public's money was not taken in a discriminatory manner that only focused on the wealthier in society.

But it's a positive and negative situation with its good and bad sides. So other observations were, yes as much as the World Cup was there, you would find in terms of attendance as well—I suppose this has to do with inequality. The average South African would probably not have been able to necessarily afford to be part of the festivities. There are many people that live in shacks and would not necessarily been able to afford to partake. So again, you would find it's the much richer, your upper-class society that would have enjoyed more, the one-on-one experience of actually being able to also go to the stadiums. (Jessica)

From Kristen's reflection, the government seems to have promised the people more than they were able to deliver.

I think when the government promoted it and justified all this spending on the event, I think people got in their minds that they were going to get so much more than they did, and I know some people got a lot out of the event, but I just felt mixed feelings. I did kind of feel that maybe someone should have explained better about what the event was going to bring as opposed to allowing the political rhetoric because people have negative associations to it now. So, if you ask someone like in the townships, they will tell you oh no, they just took our money. (Kristen)

It is clear through this extract and the reflections of the other respondents how the propaganda left the community members feeling like the World Cup was a short-lived feel-good experience, a Potemkin spectacle. It could be said that the government overpromised and underdelivered, resulting in community members questioning their trust of the government.

Conclusion

The results of this research support the idea that the desire for public diplomacy through the hosting of mega-events should not only leverage a legacy that positively showcases the host nation internationally but also hasten national redevelopment plans. The respondents articulate their experiences of regeneration projects built around the event and how these were expected to change the way of life in South Africa for the better. Taken together, the act of diplomacy and soft power was seen as a way of building South Africa's reputation through the FIFA 2010 World Cup. However, through the recollections of the respondents, this appears to have had a mixed impact. Life after the event changed, and it was not long before the imperfections began to reveal themselves. The simultaneous act of pursuing diplomacy and regeneration has been shown to affect the host community's welfare.

The question of the effectiveness of soft power as a national (re)branding and regeneration tool in the context of mega-events is raised through the respondents' lived experiences. The findings presented point out limitations to Nye's (2021) conceptualization of soft power, questioning the overall strategy of soft power as an approach that helps alter reputations in a way that favors promoting national agendas over the needs of the people. As Wolfe (2023) argues through the concept of Potemkinism, pursuing mega-events for political gain under the guise of urban development projects tends to create a superficial surface that hides a different reality underneath. Indeed, one of the limitations with Nye's explanation of soft power is that it does not explain why political gain and the diplomatic activity of nation (re)branding require a trade-off from the community. Some of these trade-offs have been articulated by the respondents as the misallocation of community resources and prioritization of governmental interests at the cost of the community's welfare.

The data in this study found an association between placing priority to changing negative perceptions of a country and how this can come at the cost of the host nation's own sense of wellbeing. Indeed, in the sociopolitical discourse of mega-event studies, it remains important to explore community experiences of mega-events from the context of developing nations. In particular, it is crucial to see how the persuasive approach to international relations through the social influence of mega-events affects community experiences and perceptions. Several questions remain unanswered at present. For instance, rather than coercion, it could be valuable to consider community engagement where the use of soft power in mega-events is concerned. This research will serve as a base for future studies that explore the roles of the host community, particularly how the community is viewed as a key stakeholder that sits outside of the government but has a specialist view that should be taken into consideration to ensure a balance of power dynamics that yields benefits for all.

REFERENCES

Andranovich, G., Burbank, M. J., & Heying, C. H. (2001). Olympic cities: Lessons learned from mega-event politics. *Journal of Urban Affairs, 23*(2), 113–131. https://doi.org/10.1111/0735-2166.00079

Cornelissen, S., & Maennig, W. (2010). On the political economy of 'feel-good' effects at sport mega-events: Experiences from FIFA Germany 2006 and prospects for South Africa 2010. *Alternation* [online], *17*(2), 96–120. https://ssrn.com/abstract=2971907

Dowse, S., & Fletcher, T. (2020). Sport mega-events, the 'non-West' and the ethics of event hosting. In *Ethical concerns in sport governance* (pp. 25–41). Routledge. https://doi.org/10.1080/17430437.2018.1401359

Gibson, O. (2014, May 9). IOC says 'totally unfeasible' for London to step in for Rio as 2016 Olympics host. *The Guardian.* Retrieved February 29, 2024, from https://www.theguardian.com/sport/2014/may/09/ioc-olympic-games-2016-host-rio-london

Grix, J., Brannagan, P. M., & Lee, D. (2019). *Entering the global arena: Emerging states, soft power strategies and sports mega-events.* Springer. https://doi.org/10.1007/978-981-13-7952-9

Maharaj, B. (2015). The turn of the south? Social and economic impacts of mega-events in India, Brazil and South Africa. *Local Economy, 1–17.* https://doi.org/10.1177/0269094215604318

Mitchell, B. (2015, June 23). 1995 Rugby World Cup: Unifying a divided nation. *ESPN.* Retrieved February 7, 2024, from http://en.espn.co.uk/southafrica/rugby/story/267173.html

Musikavanhu, R. (2019). *Fostering community support for mega-events: A narrative inquiry of stories and experiences in the context of Cape Town, South Africa.* Doctoral Thesis (Doctoral). Bournemouth University.

Nye, J. S. (2021). Soft power: The evolution of a concept. *Journal of Political Power, 14*(1), 196–208. https://doi.org/10.1080/2158379X.2021.1879572

Polkinghorne, d. E. (1995). Narrative configuration as a qualitative analysis. In J. A. Hatch & R. Wisniewski (Eds.), *Life history and narrative* (pp. 5–25). Falmer Press. https://doi.org/10.1080/0951839950080103

Rocha, C. M., Barbanti, V. J., & Chelladurai, P. (2017). Support of local residents for the 2016 Olympic Games. *Event Management, 21*(3), 251–268. https://doi.org/10.3727/152599517X14942648527491

Skey, M. (2023). Sportswashing: Media headline or analytic concept? *International Review for the Sociology of Sport, 58*(5), 749–764. https://doi.org/10.1177/10126902221113608

Van Der Merwe, J. (2007). Political analysis of South Africa's hosting of the Rugby and Cricket World Cups: Lessons for the 2010 Football World Cup and beyond? *Politikon, 34*(1), 67–81. https://doi.org/10.1080/02589340701336294

Wolfe, S. D. (2023). The juggernaut endures: Protest, Potemkinism, and Olympic reform. *Leisure Studies, 0*(0), 1–15. https://doi.org/10.1080/02614367.2023.2195201

Open Access This chapter is licensed under the terms of the Creative Commons Attribution 4.0 International License (http://creativecommons.org/licenses/by/4.0/), which permits use, sharing, adaptation, distribution and reproduction in any medium or format, as long as you give appropriate credit to the original author(s) and the source, provide a link to the Creative Commons license and indicate if changes were made.

The images or other third party material in this chapter are included in the chapter's Creative Commons license, unless indicated otherwise in a credit line to the material. If material is not included in the chapter's Creative Commons license and your intended use is not permitted by statutory regulation or exceeds the permitted use, you will need to obtain permission directly from the copyright holder.

CHAPTER 4

Behind the Golden Glow: The Soft Power, Potemkinism, and Protest of Australian Mega-Events

Max Holleran, Jennifer Minner, and Martin Abbott

Abstract As Australia looks forward to hosting the 2032 Olympics, it is an opportune time to reflect on the hard edges of mega-event soft power in the land down under, especially in relation to Brisbane's experience with Expo 88. This chapter provides a brief review of the history of Australian mega-events, including international exhibitions and the Olympic Games. It then applies a lens of Potemkinism to Brisbane, the Queensland state capital, and the surrounding region that will host the XXXV Olympiad. The golden glow associated with this event conceals a complex and contested history of neoliberal ambitions, demolition, and displacement. That Queensland is already a destination for domestic and international tourists and retirees, has not made hosting the 2032 Olympic Games any more palatable. Queensland's history of mega-events demonstrates how the state uses unique funding opportunities and moments of

---

M. Holleran (✉)
The University of Melbourne, Melbourne, Australia
e-mail: max.holleran@unimelb.edu.au

J. Minner • M. Abbott
Cornell University, Ithaca, USA

© The Author(s) 2025
S. D. Wolfe (ed.), *The Hard Edge of Soft Power*, Mega Event Planning, https://doi.org/10.1007/978-981-96-3515-3_4

regulatory power to address not only the event at hand but to execute larger priorities related to infrastructure, economic development, and land use.

Keywords Soft power • Potemkinism • Neoliberalism • Australia • Mega-events

INTRODUCTION

Mega-events project national power in pursuit of increased commercial and cultural clout abroad. From nineteenth-century international exhibitions to the Olympic Games, Australian mega-events have served as catalysts to rebrand national and city identities (Aronczyk, 2013) and accelerate urban transformations (Ganis, 2015; Goad, 2021). They have also been used to mobilize pathways for city-to-city economic cooperation and small-scale diplomacy (Acuto, 2013). While mega-events have demonstrated soft power or "the ability to affect others by attraction and persuasion rather than just coercion and payment" (Nye, 2017, p. 2), they have proven costly, controversial, and involved in the suppression of civil protest (Lenskyj, 2000; Ryan, 2018). Mega-events have been locally powerful in signifying a newly energized growth coalition that can demolish whole neighborhoods, stymie opposition, particularly anti-development activists (Lancione, 2017), and alert investors to opportunity. They have also provided a platform to broadcast protests of wider injustices and government policies and to organize for change (Neilson, 2002). Behind the alluring visage of these popular mega-events, soft power has a decidedly hard edge.

As Australia once again takes the mantle as host of the 2032 Olympics, it is an opportune time to reflect on the Potemkinism of mega-events in the land down under. Wolfe (2024: 3) describes Potemkinism as a false front or "superficial covering [that] can conceal unpleasant realities." This concept describes the contradictions between the golden glow that promotes host cities, regions, and nations that disguises the harsher reality of hosting international events of this scale (Broudehoux, 2017; Wolfe, 2024). In action, soft power is wielded not only as a force for shaping narratives to persuade international audiences. It also quells internal conflicts and discourses from within the nation (Wolfe, 2020). The locus of growing discontent is a rising awareness of the economic risks and social impacts of hosting a mega-event. How this discontent will play out ahead of the Brisbane Olympics is an open question.

To this end, this chapter examines the past and future of mega-event soft power in Australia. It does this by applying the lens of Potemkinism in Brisbane, the Queensland state capital, and the surrounding region that will host the XXXV Olympiad. Over the last half century or so, Brisbane and Queensland have been particularly active in bidding for mega-events. While the city's goal has been to harness soft power domestically and establish a global profile, Brisbane has never strayed far from controversy. In the lead up to Brisbane's Expo 88, for instance, protests were limited and deliberately muted by the government. Similarly, the Gold Coast Commonwealth games of 2018 boosted the regional unity of Southeast Queensland and its surrounding beachfront urbanization (the most concentrated touristic area in Australia). Nowadays, protesters are openly contesting how the design and planning for the Brisbane Olympics, spread regionally within the State of Queensland, should unfold. Indeed, the contention has grown into a high-profile political drama as planning efforts gear up. These protests call into question the social, economic, and sustainability promises made by the Games' boosters.

Ahead of the 2032 Olympics, this chapter argues there is a lesson in mega-event soft power that can be learned from Brisbane's past: how past and present social movements organize against a mega-event not only offers clues about the future of mega-events but also their projection of soft power. What can we learn about Potemkinism, protest, and soft power in examining the past and future of Australian mega-events? To answer this question, we draw on the history of mega-events in Australia. We then focus on Brisbane's historical and contemporary urban transformations, discussing activist opposition to Expo 88 and the forthcoming 2032 Olympics. This chapter draws from multiple sources including municipal documents, scholarly literature, local newspapers, interviews, and media including protest films.

From Nation Building and City Boosterism to Protest and Neoliberalism

Australian cities have long used mega-events, from international exhibitions to sporting events, for city boosterism. The state has employed these happenings to build a national image (Broudehoux, 2004). The history of internationally facing events in Australia extends back to nineteenth-century examples such as the Intercolonial Exhibition Sydney (1870), Sydney International Exhibition (1879), Melbourne International Exhibition (1880), and Melbourne Centennial International Exhibition (1888). These expositions created new public spaces and works, as well as constructing images of the past, prowess, and future promise of Australia. These events projected images of host cities and nation as emerging from the benefits of colonization and settler society, such as the ethnographic displays in the 1879 Sydney International Exhibition used to portray Aboriginal peoples as Other (Jones, 2016).[1]

Beginning in the 1950s, Australian cities, enriched and growing in post-World War II, began competing to host mega-events to bolster tourism and show an increased regional geopolitical role. Melbourne was the first Australian city to take the mantle as Summer Olympics host in 1956.[2] According to Davison (1997), the lead-up to the games included much contestation between those promoting modernization of Melbourne to impress an imagined international audience versus "a small but vocal minority of Labor politicians and welfare workers had opposed the Games as an unjustifiable extravagance" (p. 69) in the face of a post-war housing crisis. Internal pressure exerted by business elites to change the city to meet the requirements of an external audience was used to overcome opposition. According to Davidson: "The fear of what the world might think was a powerful weapon in the hands of local modernizers. ... 'Australia would be the laughingstock of the world if the 1956 Games were not a success', said the Melbourne businessman, K.G. Luke upon his return from the Helsinki Olympics" (p. 70). Skepticism toward the benefits of hosting versus costs would be echoed in subsequent marquee mega-events. Likewise, the gaze of the internal audience would be used to justify change in the host city and nation.

The next large-scale effort to elevate Australia on the global stage, besides the Commonwealth Games in 1982, came 32 years later. Brisbane's Expo '88 exemplified a turn toward the explicit use of mega-events in neoliberal-style planning to entice private investment through supportive

[1] The memory of this nineteenth-century mega-event and trauma inflicted on Aboriginal peoples was the center of a 2016 public art project in Sydney called *barrangal dyara (skin and bones)*. See Jones, 2016; Minner, 2019; Abbott & Minner, 2024.

[2] Australia hosted the Commonwealth Games in Sydney in 1932, Perth in 1962, Brisbane in 1982, Melbourne in 2006, and Gold Coast in 2018. Melbourne was also awarded the 2026 Commonwealth Games and later withdrew their bid.

public expenditures. It was representative of a growing trend in the 1980s to use mega-events as a tool to transition urban waterfronts from marine and industrial uses and working-class homes and businesses to new leisure spaces. This formula had been developed in earlier World Expos such as the Expo '67 in Montreal and Expo '86 in Vancouver. Organized for the year of Australia's Bicentennial, Expo 88 was also a site of Aboriginal protest against the lack of sovereignty and land rights, as well as a place of performance that celebrated Aboriginal cultures (Ryan, 2018).

Shortly thereafter, in 1993, Sydney was announced as the host of the 2000 Olympics. The Olympic Games were once again used to broadcast images of an Australian identity globally, while repositioning Australia and the Olympic Games as "green" through the high-profile clean-up of Homebush Bay. Although touted as an environmental success, there have been noted shortcomings in the environmental clean-up (Gold & Gold, 2024) as well as the suppression of protest (Lenskyj, 2000).

Neilson (2002) points out that the Olympic Games provided a global media platform by which Indigenous groups hoped to "generate international pressure that might expedite legislative or constitutional change in Australia" (p. 14). He notes:

> Contrary to mainstream belief, the protests surrounding the Sydney Olympic Games were quite successful. It is just that these activities did not take the expected form of street demonstrations, but sought rather to avoid violent conflict while working through the communicative networks of the media. (p. 13)

The enduring racial tension in Australian society was on show throughout the Sydney Olympics. The inclusion of Aboriginal performances in the Opening Ceremony and Midnight Oil's performance "Beds Are Burning" while wearing "sorry" shirts at the Closing Ceremony stirred controversy. In between, the symbolism of Cathy Freeman's gold medal performance in the 400 meters was questioned in heated discussions about identity and culture (Bruce & Wensing, 2009). The subsequent global attention spotlighted stories of Australia's Stolen Generation, lack of sovereignty, and the prime minister's refusal to apologize—Olympic spectacles cited as garnering international support that applied political pressure within Australia (Neilson, 2002).

Australian mega-events of the twentieth century took place in a somewhat more halcyon time for large outlays of public funds. Urban regeneration models, such as the 1992 Barcelona Olympics, were touted in the press, rather than the overspending, graft, and white elephant projects that would come to define the Olympic movement over the next two decades in Athens (2004), Sochi (2014), and Rio de Janeiro (2016). However, even the roaring success of Expo '88 and the 2000 Sydney Olympics were hotly contested. Activists protested the loss of community landmarks, housing, and other social, environmental, and economic costs (Lenskyj, 2000). Protesters called attention to the continued exclusion of Aboriginal peoples from the benefits of both the mega-events and the Nation as a whole. This history of protest and community organizing, whether inward facing within the host city or region, or integral to the international spectacle, is essential to understanding how mega-events shape urban growth.

Unsettling the Triumphant Tale of Brisbane's Mega-Event Past

In considering soft power and the future of mega-events in Australia, it is instructive to return to Brisbane's hosting of Expo '88. The impact of Expo 88 has been consciously revived as a success to be replicated in the lead-up to the 2032 Olympics. However, the singular positive memory of staging this event papers over a complex and contested history of neoliberal ambitions, demolition, and displacement. In this sense, mega-events serve as an act of Potemkinism, presenting a highly specific geography and moment in a city as a stand-in for the whole, one that can often be inaccurate or even misleading.

In the post-World War II era, low prices and relatively cheap housing fueled rapid growth in permanent residents at a time of corrupt state leadership under Premier Joh Bjelke-Petersen who governed from 1968 to 1987 (Sampford, 2009; Wear, 2002). In the 1980s, Brisbane was the fastest-growing Australian city (Australian Bureau of Statistics, 1996). Bjelke-Petersen worked to attract the 1982 Commonwealth Games and Expo 88; the mega-events fit into a wider strategy of quick and large-scale urbanization. These mega-events were not the cause of new development but ratified the intensive growth that came before them. However, Brisbane had only 1.2 million people in 1985, so its success in attracting mega-events shows an ability to corral federal funding at an outsized scale.

The fact that Queensland began campaigning for mega-events under the leadership of Bjelke-Petersen, later investigated for corruption (Sampford, 2009; Wear, 2002), also demonstrates how bidding, preparing, and executing these events under an international spotlight can sometimes be a substitute for democratic processes that are either moribund or non-functioning. Peterson was also instrumental in shutting down all street protests in the state from 1977 to 1979, after several more ad-hoc measures often directed at the fracas around sporting events (Heath & Burdon, 2017). As in other places heavily invested in mega-events, they can often help to expand policing powers in a state of exception and then normalize a unique moment into the status quo (Pauschinger, 2020).

In Queensland, Expo 88 came at a time of renewed cooperation between city, state, and federal government to make Brisbane a destination city for tourism and new residents. This came to the chagrin of local residents who saw mega-events as land grabs and a means to turbocharge gentrification. This was not refuted by Premier Bjelke-Petersen. Quite the contrary, Bjelke-Petersen said of the Expo:

> Goodness gracious me, there I was looking out my window at Parliament House when I saw South Brisbane and I thought: "What a good place for a land deal!", and then some bright sparks came up with a way for the government to pay for it. We have got some very free enterprise in Queensland—get yours now. (Piccini, 2016)

Bjelke-Petersen was also instrumental in turning the Gold Coast (just south of Brisbane) into Australia's major mass tourism hub. Today it is one of the most densely urbanized places in the country. The Gold Coast also hosted the 2018 Commonwealth Games, cementing the city's reputation and ability to act on the world stage, a not-so-difficult task given its abundant hotel space, famous coastline, and vertical urbanization. Bjelke-Petersen sold the greater Brisbane region to the world as an important new destination for people and capital.

The historian Jon Piccini argues that Brisbane has a long history of mobilization from Aboriginal, working class, and immigrant populations, often in the South of the City, that intensified during the 1982 Commonwealth Games. By the planning stage of the 1988 Expo, a countercultural and working-class opposition had gelled into a social movement that connected mega-events to graft. *The Cane Toad Times*, a local alternative newspaper at the time, satirized (Woodward & Pyle, 1985):

[C]ome to the banks of the muddy and chemically-tainted Brisbane River and join Queensland, Australia, the World in a no-holds barred, you-pick-up-the-cheque-and-the-Cabinet-picks-up-the-capital-gains celebration of two hundred years of opportunism, shady land deals and sharp accounting practices.

Piccini even uses the trope of developing country corruption to lacerate the pretensions of Queensland's business class attempting to enrich themselves with the public purse: "[T]he global, cultured pretensions of Expo were ill-suited to the subtropical corrupt free market paradise of Brisbane."[3] As in many other circumstances, mega-events offered a means to demonstrate newly acquired prestige but they also could be sources of international embarrassment if events were mismanaged, corruption too blatant, or facilities deemed subpar. As a fast-growing region, Queensland had the pressure not just of creating a successful international image but also of making a name for Brisbane compared to much larger, and historically wealthier, Melbourne and Sydney.

Within some accounts, the story of Expo 88 is a triumphal narrative about its host city's rise from an underdog city in the "Deep North" with its beguiling history of political corruption to the "world class city" that it has become today (Ryan, 2018). As the narrative goes, seemingly against all odds, Brisbane hosted Expo 88, a *coup de chance* for a city considered a country town with a reputation of being hopelessly provincial (Ryan, 2018). New spaces of consumption made the destruction of the South Bank and West End communities and a portion of the central business district more palatable, with the introduction in the leftover spaces of new outdoor dining opportunities, and Expo 88 is credited with the transformation of Brisbane into an al fresco dining paradise (O'Brien & Chalip, 2008). Thus, it is not only destruction but opportunities for consumption that helped to erase the more troubling history of land resumptions and demolitions.

Another dominant narrative is that the neighborhood that was to become the site for Expo 88 was derelict and blighted, and devoid of the characteristics and people of a successful world-class city. To justify redevelopment, the neighborhood was denigrated. The Expo 88 souvenir program described it as "an area of derelict dockyards, unacknowledged brothels and disreputable hotels," write Smith & Mair, 2018 who explain:

[3] Ibid.

Like many other mega-event projects and waterfront schemes, the development of Brisbane's South Bank displaced low-income groups and "scruffy" industries which were swept aside by a growth regime intent on property development and new investment. (n.p.)

Only by representing the South Bank as an area that was decaying, depraved, and worthless could such a large-scale transformation be justified (Smith and Mair (2018), np).

Essay films about Brisbane created in the years prior to Expo 88 offer counter-views.[4] These include Wendy Rogers and Sue Ward's 16 mm film *City for Sale: Images in the Modern City* (1988), Debra Beattie's *Expo Schmexpo* (1984), and Stephen Stockwell's *This City Is Dead* (1985). Archived in the Queensland State Library, on Vimeo, and on YouTube, these films directly challenge the triumphal narrative of Expo 88. Rogers and Ward's film depicts harrowing images of demolitions in preparation for the Expo, juxtaposing them with images of skyscrapers and upscale downtown shopping intended to dramatize the commercialization of Brisbane and the dispossession of its low-income residents. *Expo Schmexpo* portrays quotidian scenes of Brisbane, mourning the loss of community spaces, while lampooning political figures of that time. Stockwell's film includes an interview with Bob Weatherall, CEO of the Foundation for Aboriginal and Islander Research Action, who speaks about the significance of Musgrave Park, which was threatened by redevelopment for the Expo and was used as a site of gatherings and protests for land rights before and during Expo 88.[5] These films are part of a historical record of the strife that Expo 88 caused in the lives of the residents who were displaced for an Expo that sported a theme of leisure. The films offered insights into a countercultural scene attempting to challenge the idea that Brisbane was a city for sale to the highest bidder.

In general, the confluence of public funds and developers was of great concern to Queenslanders who had previously seen the mass urbanization of the Gold Coast with frequently lax environmental oversight. Some called this "adolescent urbanism": both a jab at its building quality and the intoxicated young spring breakers who holidayed there (Burton, 2016).

---

[4] The discussion of *City for Sale: Images in the Modern City* is elaborated upon in Abbott and Minner (2024).

[5] In addition to Musgrave Park, there were the "beats" or networks of pubs, hotels, and other community gathering spaces in this area that were important to the social life of Aboriginal community members (Greenop & Memmott, 2007).

The adoption of the "entertainment city" model of development (Clark, 2011) meant prioritizing tourism needs and cultural tastes over spaces and businesses that served longtime residents. What's more, it made clear that mega-events were land deals negotiated between a real estate power elite rather than a participatory process that listened to and acted upon the needs of residents.

Growing Storm Clouds for Brisbane's Olympic Games

The global phenomenon of rising skepticism about hosting games fueled changes to the bidding process that has affected the 2032 Olympics. Brisbane was selected as the first host city in a revamped process in which contenders save money through speedier selection rather than outright competition (Tham, 2023). New requirements for both Olympic and World Expo host cities to consider the built and social legacy of hosting in their bids have come in response to criticisms about displacement, white elephant stadia, and other social and economic costs to host cities and regions. Brisbane will also be subject to more sustainable development goals that were enacted to lessen the carbon footprint of such events (Weaver et al., 2023). Additionally, the games come at a time when the geopolitical soft power of the Olympics (Wolfe, 2020) has both renewed urgency and a growing sense of obsolescence. One might ask generally how countries can come together through sport to achieve common goals. Of the 2032 Olympics, one should ask how Brisbane and the state of Queensland more broadly will weather the internal fissures, protests, and critiques that have already begun to surface.

Urban redevelopment in the lead-up to the Games appears to echo the controversial redevelopment schemes of 1980s Brisbane. On a Queensland State Government website, the Honorable Dr. Steven Miles proclaims that a "[w]orld-class Woolloongabba revitalization kicks off," rebranding the Woolloongabba district as the "East Bank" and calling it "the largest urban renewal since South Bank" (Miles, 2023).[6] In the same government release and echoed in the press is a rendering that shows a new Olympic Stadium glowing luminously in the foreground of the Gabba Priority Redevelopment Area. A golden Brisbane River glistens in the sweaty

---

[6] The Honorable Dr. Steven Miles is described as Deputy Premier, Minister for State Development, Infrastructure, Local Government and Planning and Minister Assisting the Premier on Olympic and Paralympic Games Infrastructure.

hereafter of Olympian dreams for urban renewal. In the Priority Development Area, private land for homes and businesses can be resumed for redevelopment to accommodate the expansion of sporting facilities. In other newspaper articles and social media posts, photos show school children and parents holding protest signs questioning the fate of their school, which is a listed historic property threatened with demolition.

Rifts have grown between the Brisbane City Council and the State of Queensland over costs. Consequently, the lack of consultation (Messenger, 2024) led the Lord Mayor of Brisbane to resign from an intergovernmental committee whose charge is the organization of the 2032 Olympic Games. One major point of contention has been the proposal to tear down the existing Gabba Stadium for a new one that is the centerpiece of the East Bank plan. While protests over this are vaguely reminiscent of Expo 88, the Woolloongabba district is already much wealthier than South Bank and not the bastion of diversity and affordable housing lost in the 1980s. Additionally, heritage logics of the present include concern over the loss of embodied carbon that might otherwise be saved in a preservation scenario. More generally, Olympic projects have been widely criticized for their cost, including by the federal government, which has declined to follow through with promised funding because it accused the Queensland government of including expenses beyond the scope of the Olympics (Messenger, 2023). In another example, a proposed AU$ 100 million Whitewater Olympic venue has been criticized as a "white water elephant" that threatens koala habitat and includes "heritage-listed wells and indigenous landmark" and lands primarily designated for conservation (Kerr, 2023).

The risk of overt withdrawal from hosting mega-events may be growing in Australia. In 2023, the Premier of Victoria canceled plans to host the Commonwealth Games in Melbourne over fears of an inflated budget. By walking away, the State of Victoria lost approximately AU$ 250 million in funds already spent that could not be recovered. Indeed, the critique of cost overruns without long-term benefits has gone from an activist talking point, supported by community organizations and some residents, to a mainstream policy argument (Minnaert, 2012), with serious repercussions for the future of mega-events.

Brisbane has also seen protests against the rising expense of hosting the games amid a cost of living and housing crisis. Queensland, once a bastion of conservatism, has seen surprising electoral success in the past two elections for federal parliamentary seats taken by the Australian Green Party.

The Green Party opposed the tearing down of the Gabba Stadium and, more broadly, for taking away construction resources from building up housing stock (Smee, 2023).[7] The Queensland Green Party has also invigorated environmental protest in the city, pointing out the irony of "the most sustainable games ever" in a city with an extreme flooding problem.

While infrastructure is created for temporary events, long-term "climate proofing" has languished in Brisbane. The often-overflowing Brisbane River (Meanjin River in the language of the Indigenous Turrbal people) poses an existential threat to the city (Cook, 2019). Questions abound regarding the long-term utility of infrastructure, focus on entertainment rather than housing, and deal with politically powerful construction companies. Other more Queensland-specific problems include an overreliance on tourism and the possibility of mass flooding in the newly built precincts along the Meanjin River. Skepticism directed at mega-events has brought together three major constituencies: environmental activists, neighborhood and heritage advocates who do not want the city to be radically altered, and an interesting mix of fiscal conservatives and housing advocates (who have no issue with public spending but believe it should be for low-income housing rather than sport).

Conclusion

This chapter argued that much can be learned from past Australian mega-events, especially in reflecting on Brisbane's experiences with Expo 88, as the region and nation look forward to the 2032 Olympics. Brisbane's experience hosting Expo '88 offers clues about the future of mega-events in the city and the projection of soft power. In looking to the past, the aim should be to learn how to address the hard edges of mega-events that so often trammel the needs of local residents. Brisbane and the State Government of Queensland could do more to engage with present social movements that are organizing against sweeping redevelopment agendas.

Without considering the questionable mega-event past in Australia and in the region, any soft power benefits derived from hosting the Olympics will be tarnished. With plans to nix the demolition and rebuild the Gabba Stadium, perhaps there is hope that host city and state will bend to citizen concerns.

---

[7] Plans to tear down the stadium were scrapped in March 2024 (McKay & Stewart, 2024).

The fact that Queensland is already a hub for tourism and retirement has not made the 2032 Olympic Games more palatable. Like other places that have seen a major shift to a tourism economy, particularly mass beachfront tourism (Holleran, 2013), there is concerted local animus about prioritizing the needs of visitors over long-term residents, particularly when construction resources are limited. While those in favor of the 2032 Brisbane Olympics have attempted to make a strong economic case for improving the city's tourism infrastructure through state and federal financing (Eeles, 2023), they have been stymied by a coalition of environmentalists, neighborhood, heritage, and housing advocates. More problematically for the Olympic organizing committee, economic arguments against the mega-event have already been compelling because of major fissures between state and local government. Regulatory dysfunction has not proven that the Games are untenable, but it has cast doubt on the lasting benefits and long-term planning of the event. State and federal infighting has been mobilized as a talking point from those opposed to urban redevelopment in the name of mega-events to show that the project will not have lasting benefits and that slipshod planning will guarantee that public funds are wasted. In this sense, the spectacle of mega-events serves as a Potemkin façade to distract from more intractable issues (Wolfe, 2024).

Queensland's history of mega-events demonstrates how the state often uses unique funding opportunities and moments of regulatory power to address not only the task at hand but to execute larger priorities related to infrastructure, economic development, and land use. Sustainability goals may also be added to these moments of exception but that remains to be seen (Pauschinger, 2020). While Queensland has promised to build all 2032 structures to higher standards of energy efficiency, they have not taken advantage of accumulated planning powers to propose new master planning that addresses flooding vulnerability. As in other places where mega-events have been contested, the primacy of economic development over social and environmental goals is a standout issue and one that has caused a great deal of ire.

Acknowledgments Thanks to Dingkun Hu for his research assistance. Martin's studies at Cornell were supported generously by the John Crampton Fellowship.

References

Abbott, M., & Minner, J. (2024). The art of resisting mega-event amnesia: Reconstructing urban memory post-expo in Sydney and Brisbane. *City: Analysis of Urban Change, Theory, Action., 28*(3–4), 460–483. https://doi.org/10.1080/13604813.2024.2366119

Acuto, M. (2013). Global Cities, Governance and Diplomacy The Urban Link. Routledge.

Aronczyk, M. (2013). *Branding the nation: The global business of national identity.* Oxford University Press.

Australian Bureau of Statistics. (1996). *4102.0 - Australian Social Trends, 1996.* Retrieved March 14, 2024, from https://www.abs.gov.au/ausstats/abs@.nsf/2f762f95845417aeca25706c00834efa/924739f180990e34ca2570ec0073cdf7!OpenDocument#:~:text=Between%201986%20and%201994%20the%20fastest%20growing%20cities%20were%20Brisbane,3%25%20in%20the%20late%201980s

Broudehoux, A. (2004). *The making and selling of post-Mao Beijing. Planning, history, and the environment series.* Routledge.

Broudehoux, A. (2017). *Mega-events and urban image construction: Beijing and Rio de Janeiro.* Routledge.

Bruce, T., & Wensing, E. (2009). (2009) 'She's not one of us': Cathy Freeman and the place of Aboriginal people in Australian national culture. *Australian Aboriginal Studies, 2,* 90–100.

Burton, P. (2016). The Gold Coast as a city of 'adolescent urbanism.'. *Built Environment, 42*(1), 189–204.

City for Sale Film. (1988). *City for sale* [Film]. https://vimeo.com/143218600

Clark, T.N. Ed. (2011). *City as Entertainment Machine.* Rownman and Littlefield.

Cook, M. (2019). *A river with a city problem: A history of Brisbane floods.* University of Queensland Press.

Davison, G. (1997). Welcoming the world: The 1956 Olympic Games and the re-presentation of Melbourne. *Australian Historical Studies, 27*(109), 64–76. https://doi.org/10.1080/10314619708596043

Eeles, S. (2023). The challenge of delivering a 'climate-positive' 2032 Brisbane Olympic and Paralympic Games. *ABC News.* Retrieved January 8, 2023, from . https://www.abc.net.au/news/2023-01-08/brisbane-olympics-paralympics-2032-climate-positive-challenge/101685202

Expo Schmexpo Motion Picture. (1984). *Expo schmexpo* [Film]. https://vimeo.com/362213144

Ganis, M. (2015). *Planning urban places: Self-organising places with people in mind.* Routledge, Taylor & Francis Group.

Goad, P. (2021). Making Melbourne modern: Urban transformation and the 1956 Olympic Games. In *Proceedings of the 16th International Docomomo Conference, Inheritable resilience: Sharing values of global modernities.*

Gold, J. R., & Gold, M. M. (Eds.). (2024). *Olympic cities: City agendas, planning and the world's games, 1896–2032* (4th ed.). Routledge.

Greenop, K., & Memmott, P. (2007). Urban Aboriginal place values in Australian metropolitan cities: The case study of Brisbane. In C. L. Miller & M. M. Roche (Eds.), *Past matters: Heritage and planning history: Case studies from the Pacific Rim*. Cambridge Scholars Publishing.

Heath, M., & Burdon, P. (2017). Silencing of activism in Australian law. *Alternative Law Journal, 42*(3), 190–194. https://doi.org/10.1177/1037969X17730193

Holleran, M. (2013). Starchitects in Spain left on the plain. *Dissent, 60*(3), 5–8.

Jones, J. (2016). *Barrangal dyara (skin and bones)*. Thames & Hudson.

Kerr, J. (2023, August 22). $100m whitewater Olympic venue stirs Redland anger at Senate inquiry. *Courier Mail*. https://www.couriermail.com.au/questnews/redlands/100m-whitewater-olympic-venue-stirs-redland-anger-at-senate-inquiry/news-story/6123375fa3b61ae52ba1aede05d08fab

Lancione, M. (2017). Revitalising the uncanny: Challenging inertia in the struggle against forced evictions. *Environment and Planning D: Society and Space, 35*(6), 1012–1032. https://doi.org/10.1177/0263775817701731

Lenskyj, H. (2000). *Inside the Olympic industry: Power, politics, and activism*. SUNY Press.

McKay, J., & Stewart, R. (2024, March 22). Dumped Gabba rebuild proposal costs Queensland taxpayers $6.4 million. *Australian Broadcast Corporation*. https://www.abc.net.au/news/2024-03-22/scrapped-gabba-rebuild-plans-cost-6-million-dollars/103617278?utm_campaign=abc_news_web&utm_content=link&utm_medium=content_shared&utm_source=abc_news_web

Messenger, A. (2023, August 22). Federal government rejected Queensland's funding request for Gabba rebuild, inquiry told. *The Guardian*. https://www.theguardian.com/sport/2023/aug/22/federal-government-rejected-queenslands-funding-request-for-gabba-rebuild-inquiry-told

Messenger, A. (2024, January 18). All options on the table as review of 'divisive' Brisbane Olympics venues plan begins. *The Guardian*. https://www.theguardian.com/sport/2024/jan/18/queensland-premier-steven-miles-gabba-stadium-rebuild-2032-brisbane-olympic-games-review

Miles, [The Honourable Dr] Steven. (2023, November 24). World-class Woolloongabba revitalisation kicks off. *Queensland Government*. Retrieved March 16, 2024, from https://statements.qld.gov.au/statements/99232#:~:text=The%20largest%20urban%20renewal%20since,new%20name%20on%20the%20table

Minnaert, L. (2012). An Olympic legacy for all? The non-infrastructural outcomes of the Olympic Games for socially excluded groups (Atlanta 1996–Beijing 2008). *Tourism Management, 33*(2), 361–370. https://doi.org/10.1016/j.tourman.2011.04.005

Minner, J. (2019). Assembly and care of memory: Placing objects and hybrid media to revisit international expositions. *Curator: The Museum Journal, 62*(2), 151–176. https://doi.org/10.1111/cura.12291

Neilson, B. (2002). Bodies of protest: Performing citizenship at the 2000 Olympic Games. *Continuum, 16*(1), 13–25. https://doi.org/10.1080/10304310220120948

Nye, J. (2017). Soft power: The origins and political progress of a concept. *Palgrave Communications, 3*(1), 17008. https://doi.org/10.1057/palcomms.2017.8

O'Brien, Danny & Chalip, Laurence. (2008). Sport Events and Strategic Leveraging: Pushing Towards the Triple Bottom Line. https://doi.org/10.1079/9781845933234.0318.

Pauschinger, D. (2020). Working at the edge: Police, emotions and space in Rio de Janeiro. *Environment and Planning D: Society and Space, 38*(3), 510–527. https://doi.org/10.1177/0263775819882711

Piccini, J. (2016, May 31). "The wrong side of the river": Expo '88 and the right to the city, text of a lecture. *The Word from Struggle Street.* https://thewordfromstrugglestreet.wordpress.com/2016/06/01/the-wrong-side-of-the-river-expo-88-and-the-right-to-the-city/

Ryan, J. (2018). *We'll show the world: Expo 88—Brisbane's almighty struggle for a little bit of cred.* University of Queensland Press.

Sampford, C. (2009). From deep north to international governance exemplar: Fitzgerald's impact on the international anti-corruption movement. *Griffith Law Review, 18*(3), 559–575. https://doi.org/10.1080/10854655.2009.10854655

Smee, B. (2023, October 25). Brisbane Greens vow to oppose 2032 Olympics at council election as Gabba stoush escalates. *The Guardian.* https://www.theguardian.com/australia-news/2023/oct/25/brisbane-greens-oppose-2032-olympic-games-gabba-jonathan-sriranganathan-city-council-election

Smith, A., & Mair, J. (2018, April 30). The making of a city: How Expo 88 changed Brisbane forever. *The Conversation.* https://theconversation.com/celebrate-88-the-world-expo-reshaped-brisbane-because-no-one-wanted-the-party-to-end-95430.

Tham, A. (2023). Getting a head start: The 2032 Olympic Movement through the preferred candidature bid involving Brisbane. *Australia. Sport in Society, 26*(3), 536–552. https://doi.org/10.1080/17430437.2022.2033222

This City is Dead. (1985). *This city is dead* [Film]. Available in two parts on YouTube: https://www.youtube.com/watch?v=kvFn0dfOZ4g [Part 1] and https://www.youtube.com/watch?v=J0-zl4-1wVs [Part 2].
Wear, R. (2002). *Johannes Bjelke-Petersen: The Lord's premier*. University of Queensland Press.
Weaver, D. B., McLennan, C.-L., Moyle, B., & Casali, L. (2023). Early resident support for a mega-event: Evidence from the 2032 Brisbane Summer Olympic Games. *Event Management, 27*(6), 967–985. https://doi.org/10.372 7/152599523X16842083117783
Wolfe, S. D. (2020). 'For the benefit of our nation': Unstable soft power in the 2018 men's World Cup in Russia. *International Journal of Sport Policy and Politics, 12*(4), 545–561. https://doi.org/10.1080/19406940.2020.1839532
Wolfe, S. D. (2024). The juggernaut endures: Protest, Potemkinism, and Olympic reform. *Leisure Studies, 43*(1), 1–15. https://doi.org/10.1080/0261436 7.2023.2195201
Woodward, L., & Pyle, D. (1985, Spring). Wrexpo 88: Making money and ensuring plenty of leisure in the age of technology. *Cane Toad Times*. https://espace. library.uq.edu.au/data/UQ_357366/Cane_Toad_Times2_03.pdf?

Open Access This chapter is licensed under the terms of the Creative Commons Attribution 4.0 International License (http://creativecommons.org/licenses/by/4.0/), which permits use, sharing, adaptation, distribution and reproduction in any medium or format, as long as you give appropriate credit to the original author(s) and the source, provide a link to the Creative Commons license and indicate if changes were made.

The images or other third party material in this chapter are included in the chapter's Creative Commons license, unless indicated otherwise in a credit line to the material. If material is not included in the chapter's Creative Commons license and your intended use is not permitted by statutory regulation or exceeds the permitted use, you will need to obtain permission directly from the copyright holder.

CHAPTER 5

Stepping Out of the Shadows: The Role of Pivotal Individuals in Qatar's Aspirations to Host Mega-Events

Tobias Zumbraegel and Sebastian Sons

Abstract The so-called Arab Spring fundamentally transformed the geographical region of West Asia and North Africa. Previous key players like Egypt and Syria lost power, while Iraq suffered from domestic conflicts and civil war as a consequence of the US-led invasion in 2003 and the disastrous postconflict management. These developments offered an opportunity for the Arab Gulf states, especially for smaller states which previously had been known for mediating international conflicts (e.g., Qatar, Kuwait, Oman) or sparkling and buzzling metropolises (e.g., the United Arab Emirates and its "Dubai Model"). These states increasingly used their influence and capacities to exert their vision over the broader region and beyond. By hosting mega-events, the Gulf monarchies aim to enhance their international credibility, engage in nation branding, and

T. Zumbraegel (✉)
University of Heidelberg, Heidelberg, Germany
e-mail: tobias.zumbraegel@uni-heidelberg.de

S. Sons
Center for Applied Research in Partnership with the Orient (CARPO), Bonn, Germany

© The Author(s) 2025
S. D. Wolfe (ed.), *The Hard Edge of Soft Power*, Mega Event Planning, https://doi.org/10.1007/978-981-96-3515-3_5

foster national identity and nationalism, all while obscuring deeper authoritarian forces behind Potemkin façades. This chapter focuses on key elites that played a crucial role in organizing two mega-events in Qatar: the climate summit (COP18) in 2012 and the FIFA World Cup 2022. In so doing, the chapter contributes to a deeper understanding that specific influential figures matter more than previously acknowledged in scholarly discussions.

Keywords Soft power • Potemkinism • Authoritarianism • Qatar • COP • Football World Cup

Introduction

Mega-events such as the FIFA World Cup 2022 in Qatar, the EXPO 2020 in Dubai, or the global climate summits in the United Arab Emirates (UAE) in 2023 and Qatar in 2012, all form an integral part of the Gulf microstates' soft power approach and should be considered as driving forces in nation branding and authoritarian power consolidation (Brannagan & Giulianotti, 2014; Brannagan & Reiche, 2022).

We present a perspective distinct from the literature on soft power in the Gulf states, demonstrating the significance of specific individuals connected to mega-events. These key figures play pivotal roles in determining whether citizens and the international community approve of the mega-event. We explore how these individuals shape mega-events in order to promote individual reputations on national and international levels, and consolidate power in complex power structures. Under a Potemkin façade, they effectively divert attention from "bad governance" while promoting an alternative, non-democratic model of success. In this context, it can be viewed as one element of a broader strategy aimed at gradually undermining and eroding the democratic-led international order through various authoritarian practices (Glasius, 2023; Kneuer & Demmelhuber, 2024; Wolfe, 2025).

So far, scholarship has not unpacked the elite-to-elite or personal relation dynamics in soft power. Hence, there is a lack of elite agency as a major aspect of decision-making processes and changing dynamics over time. Certainly, research has investigated the roles and dynamics of key stakeholders and special groups such as businessmen/merchants (Crystal, 1990; Kamrava, 2017), consultants/advisors (Ansari & Werenfels, 2023), policymakers, royals, bureaucrats (Herb, 2009; Hertog, 2010), Islamists, and tribesmen (Freer, 2019). Transnational elite networks have also received attention (Gurol et al., 2023). However, this research tends to focus on patterns of co-optation, undermining the influence of actors outside the closest circle of policymaking. We also notice that second-tier elites, specialized technocrats (*mudarā' fi-l-dawla*) from different strata of society, can play a considerable role in decision-making and in fostering authoritarian state structures. On this foundation we investigate two mega-events in the Gulf: the climate summit COP18 in 2012 and the FIFA World Cup 2022, both in Qatar.

THE NOT-SO-NEW RELEVANCE OF HOSTING MEGA-EVENTS

The Gulf states have applied numerous soft power strategies including generous foreign investments and aid initiatives, engaging in mediation, and backing international museums and higher education institutions (Kamrava, 2015; Koch, 2018; Krzymowski, 2020; Zaabi & Awamleh, 2019). In addition, organizing humanitarian conferences, promoting arts festivals, and vying for global sports events have all been key instruments (Hertog, 2017; Coates Ulrichsen, 2021). Examples include the UAE hosting the 2006 Asian Games, the 2015 FIFA Under-17 World Cup, and the 17th AFC Asian Cup in 2019. Between 2009 and 2016, it also staged the Abu Dhabi Grand Prix (Antwi-Boateng & Alhashmi, 2022), and plans to host the Asian Games again in 2030. Meanwhile, Qatar hosted the WTO Ministerial Conference in 2001, the XV Asian Games in 2006, and the COP18 in 2012 (Antwi-Boateng, 2013). Qatar has emerged as a powerhouse in international sport politics and considers mega-events as a cornerstone of its soft power policy.

Early discussions concerning economic motives for these policies have given way to more politically oriented explanations, focusing on elite-rent seeking, loyalty and legitimacy, and particularly the pursuit of recognition (Hertog, 2017). The concept of branding has been linked to soft power, as both pivot around a nation's global interests (Rookwood, 2019). Most research has centered on mega-events and place branding, contributing to external recognition (Hazime, 2011; Peterson, 2006; Sim, 2012; Theodoropoulou & Alos, 2020). Especially the FIFA World Cup in Qatar in 2022 received widespread attention (Rookwood, 2019; Scharfenort, 2014). Other works discuss the UAE's hosting of the EXPO (Koch, 2022) and Saudi Arabia's new NEOM project, which will also host mega-events such as the Asian Winter Games in 2029 (Aly, 2019, 2023).

In short, scholarship has stressed that the ambitions for global soft power by the Gulf monarchies set them apart from other smaller nations due to their magnitude and reach (Hertog, 2017). Mega-events have played a significant role in this strategy for some time, but their scale and scope are increasing. Against this backdrop, we focus on two cases in Qatar: COP18 in 2012 and the 2022 FIFA World Cup. Both events symbolize Qatar's emergence as a hub for mega-events as well as its rising political, economic, and cultural relevance. Additionally, they showcase the influence of powerful individuals who established themselves as 'faces of prominence' to promote Qatar's role as a host while functioning as cornerstones of the authoritarian system. The architect of COP18 was Abdullah bin Hamad al-Attiyah, Qatar's long-time minister of energy and industry (1992–2011), while the World Cup 2022 was associated with the popularity of Qatar's Emir Tamim bin Hamad Al Thani.

Case Studies

Qatar: COP18 in 2012

Between November 26 and December 7, 2012, Qatar hosted the eighteenth session of the Conference of the Parties (COP18) under the umbrella of the United Nations Framework Convention for Climate Change. It was the first time that the globe's largest climate gathering took place in the Arab world. The Qatar National Convention Centre, established as a sustainable planning project, served as the venue. Previously, Qatar had not been known as a green advocate. Quite the contrary, unsustainable development projects, one of the world's highest consumption habits, and largest carbon footprint (per capita) presented Qatar as a "haven of ecocide" (Luomi, 2012, p. 45). Thus, the country's new environmentally friendly orientation sparked controversy (Zumbraegel, 2019). For many observers it came as a surprise when Qatar won the bid (Luomi, 2012).

In this regard, some saw hosting as another part of Qatar's broader branding strategy (Windecker & Sendrowicz, 2014), while others blended criticism with concerns about corruption and human rights violations linked to the World Cup (Koch, 2014, p. 1120). It was perceived that holding the climate conference in this country "might seem like a joke" (Harvey, 2012), like "McDonald's hosting a conference on obesity" (Aljazeera, 2012a). An environmental activist declared that "having one of the OPEC leaders in charge of climate talks is like asking Dracula to look after a blood bank" (The Denver Post, 2012).

To address this criticism and present itself as a reliable host, Qatar created an authentic external climate policy. The government established a task force and dramatically increased the number of staff at the Ministry of Environment. Moreover, several small-scale renewable energy projects and various climate initiatives addressing ecosystem conservation, energy efficiency, and awareness campaigns were implemented. Regrettably, these efforts did not yield a lasting impact, but rather were a Potemkin façade that lacked both durability and substance. Shortly after their introduction, the situation regressed to its former patterns of unsustainability (Zumbraegel, 2022).

Still, the conference was not a failure for Qatar's reputation. The decisions framed as the Doha Climate Gateway yielded modest progress on international efforts for adapting to climate change (Carbon Trust, 2013). Primarily, this achievement can be attributed to the COP chairman, Abdullah bin Hamad al-Attiyah, one of the most noteworthy figures outside the royal circle (Kamrava, 2015; Luomi, 2012). Al-Attiyah stems from an influential Qatari family, which even asserted claims to the throne during the pre-state era. His relationship with the former Emir Hamad was described as "fierce loyalty" (Kamrava, 2015, p. 120), probably because both have been friends since childhood.

Prior to the COP presidency, he was Minister of Energy (1992–2011) and held various roles including Deputy Prime Minister (2007–2011), Director of Qatar Petroleum, and much more (Kamrava, 2015, p. 117; Luomi, 2012, p. 157). In 2006, he served as the Chairman of the United Nations Commission on Sustainable Development, where he guided global efforts toward the Sustainable Development Goals (Zumbraegel, 2022). There, he expanded his network of contacts and honed his skills in consensus-building over climate debates—both core elements that he drew upon as COP president.

Leading up to the conference, Al-Attiyah visited India, China, Iran, Ecuador, Denmark, and Germany, and even encouraged Japan, Canada, and the United States to return to the negotiating table to sign the Kyoto Protocol (Zumbraegel, 2019, 2022). At the same time, he was well-suited to advocate for Qatar's stance in international climate discussions, given his decades of experience in the oil and gas industry. He shaped the discourse in favor of Qatar in at least three ways (see Zumbraegel, 2019).

First, he stressed his country's commitment to climate change and sustainable development that launched long before the COP18. In his inaugural speech, he emphasized that Qatar is exceptionally susceptible to the impacts of climate change and stated, "[E]nvironmental sustainability stands as a fundamental pillar of our [Qatari] national vision" (Aljazeera, 2012b). Second, he relativized the environmental impact of Qatar's gas industry by reminding that gas processing results in fewer emissions compared to coal or oil. Finally, he downplayed Qatar's overall climate damage because fossil energy is used only to a limited extent within the country due to its small population. Furthermore, the dry desert state has no opportunity to offset emissions through forests. Therefore, he also deemed the presentation of emissions per capita as misleading when applied to smaller states like Qatar. Instead, he suggested to "concentrate on the amount from each country," and the big emitters such as China, India, or the United States (Harvey, 2012).

As the climate conference yielded no results, al-Attiyah pressed for outcomes through a somewhat controversial voting process, swiftly accepting the compromise proposals in the absence of objections (Fuhr & Schalatek, 2012). Following this, al-Attiyah considered COP18 a success, declaring that Qatar proved to the world that "we are fully committed to resolutions and reducing emissions" (The Business Year, 2013). After the conference, al-Attiyah largely withdrew from active politics. In 2015, he founded the *Abdullah bin Hamad Al Attiyah International Foundation for Energy and Sustainable Development*. Al-Attiyah's think tank contributes to Qatar's energy and sustainability transformation, while positioning him as a proactive, engaged, and influential voice.

Overall, Al-Attiyah can be considered a second-tier elite, a specialized technocrat (*mudarā' fi-l-dawla*). However, his personal relationship to the Emir provided him with disproportional power to affect national and supranational political outcomes. At the same time, he represents the old establishment, and with the change of power in 2013, a generation of younger technocrats also emerged. Al-Attiyah exemplifies the crucial role of non-royal technocrats in shaping the course of an authoritarian country that lacks input legitimacy (Schlumberger, 2010). However, his case also reveals the constraints in bolstering certain elites outside the royal family. Before becoming too powerful, influential figures are frequently replaced, making elite rotation a favorable strategy among autocrats (Demmelhuber & Sturm, 2021).

Qatar: FIFA World Cup

The World Cup 2022 reflected Qatar's aspirations to carry out nation branding "through the strategic leveraging of soft power" (Mohammadzadeh, 2017, p. 27), and as a diplomacy tool (Rookwood, 2019) driven by "beauty, brilliance, and benignity" (Vuving, 2009, p. 8). "Beauty" refers to a state's values and visions. "Brilliance" refers to economic diversification and political partnership. Finally, "benignity" aims to establish networks as the state presents itself through kindness as a generous, supportive, and respectful player in the global community. For Qatar as World Cup host, these motivations projected soft power in order to preserve political stability, promote economic growth, and seek leverage in international politics.

However, such aspirations were challenged by growing criticism. This oftentimes polemical debate was driven on the one hand by a critical position among some European fans, politicians, human rights activists, and parts of the media. Furthermore, some South Asian countries of migrants' origin such as India or Nepal criticized the structural violence against their nationals. On the other hand, defenders of the World Cup saw the accusations as an Islamophobic and arrogant defamation campaign, characterized by double standards (Nereim, 2022), hypocrisy (Fernández, 2022), and Eurocentrism (Fadila, 2022).

The critical debate on the World Cup in Qatar focused on: (1) human rights and migration, (2) football tradition, and (3) corruption. All three dimensions undermined Qatar's motivation to establish itself as a "champion of excellence" and promote its "virtual enlargement" (Chong, 2010; Cooper & Shaw, 2009) through the World Cup. While Qatar under the former Emir Hamad bin Khalifa Al Thani (r. 1995–2013) widely ignored such opposition and framed it as meddling in internal affairs, the Qatari leadership under the new Emir Tamim changed strategy in 2017. Since then, numerous initiatives were introduced to improve conditions for labor migrants working in Qatar who suffer from structural violence and systemic exploitation.

The recruitment of foreign workers increased Qatar's population from 50,000 in the 1950s to 1.7 million in 2010, the year the World Cup was awarded. In 2022, the population was around 2.8 million, with almost 88% coming from abroad. A "dual society" (Fargues, 2011, p. 277) developed in which most nationals were employed in the public sector and benefited from state amenities such as free healthcare and education and no taxes, while foreign workers are excluded and generally have no opportunities to obtain Qatari citizenship. Labor migrants from Asia and Africa are routinely stigmatized as a threat to national identity (Fargues & Shah, 2018, p. 1) and exempt from legal equality (AlShehabi, 2015, p. 28). As part of this "negative othering" (Palik, 2018, p. 106), migrant workers are also blamed for the lack of jobs and rising crime rates, as well burdening the economy (Falk, 2016, p. 172).

To improve this situation, Qatar announced in October 2017 that it would abolish the *kafala* (sponsorship) system, allowing workers to change employers and travel abroad without consent (HRW, 2020a). Between September 2020 and October 2023, more than 1 million applications were submitted to change their sponsors, of which more than 670,000 were approved (ILO, 2023). Employment rights have been simplified for workers and confiscation of passports is now only permitted with the written consent of the migrant worker. These regulations were also extended to domestic workers (HRW, 2020b). Cooperation with the International Labor Organization (ILO) was expanded when it opened its Doha office in April 2018, the first in the Gulf. Through these initiatives, Qatar attempted to present itself as a constructive partner and a "good global citizen" (Bianco & Sons, 2023) in order to prevent jeopardizing the World Cup. Despite such legal reforms, implementation is still insufficient and criticism from Western media continued, including discussions of "soft disempowerment" (Brannagan & Giulianotti, 2015) and accusations of sportswashing.

Qatar's Emir Tamim played a key role in organizing and hosting the World Cup. Even before he became Emir, he was involved in the World Cup bid on behalf of his father Hamad. He positioned himself within global sport diplomacy by successfully organizing the 2006 Asian Games, heading the National Olympic Committee, and acquiring the French football club Paris Saint-Germain in 2010. Against this backdrop, organizing the World Cup consolidated his reputation as a leader in regional and domestic affairs. It was speculated that the "Gulf crisis" from June 2017 to January 2021 (Coates Ulrichsen, 2020) was initiated by the blockading quartet of Saudi Arabia, the UAE, Bahrain, and Egypt to force Qatar to abandon aspirations of hosting the World Cup alone. Rather than succumbing, however, the Qatari leadership "doubled down on their pursuit of international prestige" (Bianco & Sons, 2023, p. 93).

In a speech on October 24, 2022, a few weeks before the start of the World Cup, Emir Tamim criticized an "unprecedented campaign that no host country has ever experienced." He continued that "it soon became clear to us that the campaign continues, expands and includes fabrication and double standards, until it reached a level of ferocity that made many question, unfortunately, about the real reasons and motives behind this campaign" (Aljazeera, 2022). In doing so, he presented himself as the guardian of Qatar and as a counterweight in the anti-World Cup debate from many parts of Europe.

Tamim's speech symbolizes his successful power consolidation as the undisputed leader in Qatar. He presented the World Cup as a symbol for the growing role of non-Western countries such as Qatar in a multipolar world. Since the "Gulf crisis," Tamim has been recognized by much of the population as the victorious defender of the Qatari nation against the blockading quartet. This led to a "hashtag unity" (Oruc, 2019) reflected in solidarity campaigns for the Emir on social media such as #qatarisnotalone, #istandwithqatar, #WeAreQatar, and #TamimtheGlorious (Dogan Akkas & Camden, 2020). His popularity took on the characteristics of a personality cult that glorified him as *Tamim Al-Majed* ("Tamim the Glorious") (Daily Sabah, 2017), and his World Cup speech should be understood as a continuing instrument of the Emir's general "strategic communication" (Brannagan & Reiche, 2022, p. 91).

This approach was further reflected in the ceremony after the tournament's final: after Argentina's victory over France, Tamim presented the Argentinian superstar Lionel Messi with the Arab robe of honor, the *Bisht*. The iconic image of Messi in a black robe surrounded by his celebrating teammates circled the globe and sparked controversy. While large parts of Arab societies celebrated the Emir's gesture as a respectful homage, it was framed by critical audiences as Qatar's latest attempt to instrumentalize the World Cup for a political image campaign (Church, 2023). It can be argued that the *Bisht* gesture was a final soft power message sent to an Arab audience to present Qatar as a representative of the "Arab football family" to which even international non-Arab and non-Muslim superstars such as Messi could belong.

Conclusion

Mega-events play a significant role in the transformation of power structures and decision-making in the Arab Gulf states. Hosting not only aims to enhance nation branding and soft power projection but also serves as a platform for prominent individuals to promote their public and political leverage, and create personal and institutional networks in niches such as climate or sports diplomacy. In this regard, such personalities promote authoritarian political functioning to gain soft and hard power leverages on selected global audiences. At the same time, this strategy helps to portray countries such as Qatar, despite its high level of authoritarianism, as "the good guy" and "a reliable partner."

Small Gulf states like Qatar instrumentalize mega-events to promote their ambitions as centers of "beauty, brilliance, and benignity," and boost the credibility and prominence of particular personalities. Despite the fact that events can spur international backlash, they also create opportunities to establish counter-narratives that promote social cohesion and national and regional unity. For instance, Tamim's speech created a rally-around-the-flag patriotism that addressed not only Qatari society but also the so-called Global South. He promoted a counter-narrative against the double standards of the (democratic) West and portrayed himself as a representative of non-Western societies. The debate about the World Cup thus provided Tamim an opportunity to preserve his legitimacy and personal reputation by creating a common sense of national and pan-Arab unity versus the negative discourses taking place in parts of European countries.

Mega-events provide influential stakeholders the opportunity to spread strategic messages in order to project individual and collective power, seek leverage, and promote virtual enlargement. In times of growing global polarization, such events could become even more relevant to promote hyper-nationalist narratives and consolidate leadership reputation, legitimacy, and power. As indicated by COP18 and the World Cup 2022, Qatar has emerged as a significant soft power player, using mega-events to preserve territorial integrity, political stability, legitimacy, strategic autonomy, and to promote economic diversification and nation branding. This was not possible without the involvement of charismatic figures within and outside the ruling elites at crucial junctures.

Qatar aims to find a niche in the region through mega-events, addressing growing political and economic competition with Saudi Arabia and the United Arab Emirates (UAE). The UAE has already established itself as a host country for international mega-events such as COP28 in 2023, while Saudi Arabia has successfully bided for the Asian Winter Games 2029, EXPO 2030, and the FIFA World Cup 2034. Mega-events feature prominently in the Gulf monarchies' soft power portfolio in order to attract international visitors, create global attention, and promote their respective business models. As Qatar, the UAE, and to a larger extent

Saudi Arabia are following similar mega-event strategies, growing competition but also enhanced cross-regional cooperation could become more likely. It will also be important to study these events with a view toward the prominent figures who play key roles in their planning and development.

REFERENCES

Aljazeera. (2012a, November 25). Qatar hosts climate summit amid criticism. https://www.aljazeera.com/news/2012/11/25/qatar-hosts-climate-summit-amid-criticism

Aljazeera. (2012b, November 26). Qatar hosts 'critical' climate talks. https://www.aljazeera.com/news/2012/11/26/qatar-hosts-critical-climate-talks

Aljazeera. (2022, October 25). Qatar emir slams 'ferocious' campaign against World Cup host. https://www.aljazeera.com/news/2022/10/25/qatar-emir-slams-unprecedented-campaign-against-world-cup-hosts

AlShehabi, O. (2015). Histories of migration to the Gulf. In A. Khalaf, O. AlShehabi, & A. Hanieh (Eds.), *Transit states: Labour, migration and citizenship in the Gulf* (pp. 3–38). Pluto Press.

Aly, H. (2019). Royal dream: City branding and Saudi Arabia's NEOM. *Middle East—Topics & Arguments, 12*(1), 99–109. https://doi.org/10.17192/META.2019.12.7937

Aly, H. (2023). Place branding as a political act: Approaching Saudi Arabia's NEOM beyond its shiny façade. In S. Wippel (Ed.), *Branding the Middle East* (pp. 543–560). De Gruyter. https://doi.org/10.1515/9783110741100-032

Ansari, D., & Werenfels, I. (2023). *Shadow players: Western consultancies in the Arab World: How multinational consulting firms shape public policy.* https://doi.org/10.18449/2023A53

Antwi-Boateng, O. (2013). The rise of Qatar as a soft power and the challenges. *European Scientific Journal, 2*(31), 350–368.

Antwi-Boateng, O., & Alhashmi, A. A. (2022). The emergence of The United Arab Emirates as a global soft power: Current strategies and future challenges. *Economic and Political Studies, 10*(2), 208–227. https://doi.org/10.1080/20954816.2021.1951481

Bianco, C., & Sons, S. (2023). More than a game: Football and soft power in the Gulf. *International Spectator, 58*(2), 92–106.

Brannagan, P., & Giulianotti, R. (2014). Qatar, global sport, and the 2022 FIFA World Cup. In J. Grix (Ed.), *Leveraging legacies from sports mega-events* (pp. 154–165). Palgrave Macmillan.

Brannagan, P., & Reiche, D. (2022). *Qatar and the 2022 FIFA World Cup: Politics, controversy, change.* Springer.

Brannagan, P. M., & Giulianotti, R. (2015). Soft power and soft disempowerment: Qatar, global sport, and football's 2022 World Cup finals. *Leisure Studies*, *34*(6), 703–719.
Carbon Trust. (2013). Doha: It kept the show on the road—but only just. https://www.carbontrust.com/news-and-insights/insights/doha-it-kept-the-show-on-the-road-but-only-just
Chong, A. (2010). Small state soft power strategies: Virtual enlargement in the cases of the Vatican City State and Singapore. *Cambridge Review of International Affairs*, *23*(3), 383–405.
Church, B. (2023, February 28). Reaction to Lionel Messi wearing a bisht while lifting the World Cup trophy shows cultural fault lines of Qatar 2022. *CNN*. https://edition.cnn.com/2022/12/19/football/lionel-messi-bisht-world-cup-trophy-lift-spt-intl/index.html
Coates Ulrichsen, K. (2020). *Qatar and the Gulf crisis*. Oxford University Press.
Coates Ulrichsen, K. (2021). Cultural and religious diplomacy as soft power in EU-GCC relations. In A. Abdel Ghafar & S. Colombo (Eds.), *The European Union and the Gulf Cooperation Council: Towards a new path* (pp. 57–78). Palgrave Macmillan.
Cooper, A. F., & Shaw, T. (2009). *The diplomacies of small states*. Palgrave Macmillan.
Crystal, J. (1990). *Oil and politics in the Gulf: Rulers and merchants in Kuwait and Qatar* (Vol. 24). Cambridge University Press.
Daily Sabah. (2017, August 5). With Qatar in crisis, 'Tamim the Glorious' rises as national emblem. https://www.dailysabah.com/arts-culture/2017/08/05/with-qatar-in-crisis-tamim-the-glorious-rises-as-national-emblem
Demmelhuber, T., & Sturm, R. (2021). *Decentralization in the Middle East and North Africa: Informal politics, subnational governance, and the periphery*. Nomos.
Dogan Akkas, B., & Camden, G. (2020). Political Culture in Qatar: State-Society Relations and National Identity in Transformation. In M. Karolak & N. Allam (Hrsg.), Gulf Cooperation Council Culture and Identities in the New Millennium (S. 53–73). Springer Nature Singapore. https://doi.org/10.1007/978-981-15-1529-3_4
Fadila, H. (2022, December 3). Qatar World Cup: The West's Eurocentric and Orientalist view. *Daily Sabah*. https://www.dailysabah.com/opinion/op-ed/qatar-world-cup-the-wests-eurocentric-and-orientalist-view
Falk, D. (2016). *Migranten im Spiegel der arabischen Presse. Der Einwanderungsdiskurs der arabischen Golfstaaten am Beispiel der Vereinigten Arabischen Emirate* (in German). unpublished PhD thesis. Leipzig, University of Leipzig.

Fargues, P. (2011). Immigration without inclusion: Non-nationals in nation-building in the Gulf states. *Asian and Pacific Migration Journal, 20*(3–4), 273–292.
Fargues, P., & Shah, N. M. (2018). Introduction: Migration policies, between domestic politics and international relations. In P. Fargues & N. M. Shah (Eds.), *Migration to the Gulf: Policies in sending and receiving countries* (pp. 1–17). Gulf Research Center.
Fernández, N. (2022, November 28). The massive hypocrisy of the West's World Cup 'concerns'. *Aljazeera*.
Freer, C. (2019). Clients or challengers? Tribal constituents in Kuwait, Qatar, and the UAE. *British Journal of Middle Eastern Studies*, 1–20. https://doi.org/10.1080/13530194.2019.1605881
Fuhr, L., & Schalatek, L. (2012). The "Doha Climate Gateway": Will the camel go through the eye of the needle? An analysis of the outcome of the UN Climate Change Conference (COP 18) in Doha, Qatar. Heinrich Böll Stiftung.
Glasius, M. (2023). *Authoritarian practices in a global age*. Oxford University Press.
Government Communication Office. (n.d.). Labour reform. https://www.gco.gov.qa/en/focus/labour-reform/
Gurol, J., Zumbrägel, T., & Demmelhuber, T. (2023). Elite networks and the transregional dimension of authoritarianism: Sino-Emirati relations in times of a global pandemic. *Journal of Contemporary China, 32*(139), 138–151. https://doi.org/10.1080/10670564.2022.2052444
Harvey, F. (2012, November 28). Doha: A strange place to host a climate-change conference. *The Guardian*. https://www.theguardian.com/environment/shortcuts/2012/nov/28/doha-strange-place-climate-change-conference
Hazime, H. (2011). From city branding to e-brands in developing countries: An approach to Qatar and Abu Dhabi. *African Journal of Business Management, 5*(12), 4731–4745. https://doi.org/10.5897/AJBM10.533
Herb, M. (2009). A nation of bureaucrats: Political participation and economic diversification in Kuwait and The United Arab Emirates. *International Journal of Middle East Studies, 41*(3), 375–395. https://doi.org/10.1017/S0020743809091119
Hertog, S. (2007). Segmented clientelism: The political economy of Saudi economic reform efforts. In P. Aarts & G. Nonneman (Eds.), *Saudi Arabia in the balance: Political economy, society, foreign affairs* (pp. 111–143). NYU Press.
Hertog, S. (2010). *Princes, brokers, and bureaucrats: Oil and the state in Saudi Arabia*. Cornell University Press.
Hertog, S. (2017). *A quest for significance: Gulf oil monarchies' international "soft power" strategies and their local urban dimensions* (Vol. No. 42). The London School of Economics and Political Science. http://eprints.lse.ac.uk/69883/1/Hertog_42_2017.pdf

Human Rights Watch. (2020a, January 20). *Qatar: End of abusive exit permits for most migrant workers*. https://www.hrw.org/news/2020/01/20/qatar-end-abusive-exit-permits-most-migrant-workers

Human Rights Watch. (2020b, August 24). *"How can we work without wages?" Salary abuses facing migrant workers ahead of Qatar's FIFA World Cup 2022*. https://www.hrw.org/report/2020/08/24/how-can-we-work-without-wages/salary-abuses-facing-migrant-workers-ahead-qatars

International Labour Organization. (2023, November). *Progress report on the technical cooperation programme between the Government of Qatar and the ILO*. https://www.ilo.org/wcmsp5/groups/public/%2D%2D-arabstates/%2D%2D-ro-beirut/%2D%2D-ilo-qatar/documents/publication/wcms_901686.pdf

Kamrava, M. (2015). *Qatar: Small state, big politics*. Cornell University Press.

Kamrava, M. (2017). State-business relations and clientelism in Qatar. *Journal of Arabian Studies, 7*(1), 1–27. https://doi.org/10.1080/21534764.2017.1288420

Kamrava, M., Nonnemann, G., Nosova, A., & Valeri, M. (2016). *Ruling families and business elites in the Gulf monarchies: Ever closer?* Chatham House.

Kneuer, M., & Demmelhuber, T. (2024). The international order and autocratization. In A. Croissant & L. Tomini (Eds.), *The routledge handbook of autocratization* (S. 239–249). Routledge.

Koch, N. (2014). "Building glass refrigerators in the desert": Discourses of urban sustainability and nation building in Qatar. *Urban Geography, 35*(8), 1118–1139. https://doi.org/10.1080/02723638.2014.952538

Koch, N. (2018). The geopolitics of sport beyond soft power: Event ethnography and the 2016 cycling world championships in Qatar. *Sport in Society, 21*(12), 2010–2031. https://doi.org/10.1080/17430437.2018.1487403

Koch, N. (2022). The state fetish: Producing the territorial state system at a world's fair. *Focus on Geography, 65*. https://doi.org/10.21690/foge/2022.65.2p

Krzymowski, A. (2020). The European Union and The United Arab Emirates as civilian and soft powers engaged in sustainable development goals. *Journal of International Studies, 13*(3), 41–58. https://doi.org/10.14254/2071-8330.2020/13-3/3

Luomi, M. (2012). *The Gulf monarchies and climate change: Abu Dhabi and Qatar in an era of natural unsustainability*. Hurst Company.

Mohammadzadeh, B. (2017). Status and foreign policy change in small states: Qatar's emergence in perspective. *The International Spectator, 52*(2), 19–36.

Nereim, V. (2022, November 25). Qataris bristle at what they see as double standards over their World Cup. *The New York Times*. https://www.nytimes.com/2022/11/25/world/middleeast/qatar-world-cup-criticism.html

Oruc, N. (2019). Hashtag unity: Qatar's digital nationalism in the Gulf crisis. *Journal of Arab & Muslim Media Research, 12*(1), 43–65.

Palik, J. (2018). The challenges of dual societies: The interaction of workforce nationalization and national identity construction through the comparative case studies of Saudisation and Emiratisation. In P. Fargues & N. M. Shah (Eds.), *Migration to the Gulf: Policies in sending and receiving countries* (pp. 105–125). Gulf Research Center.

Peterson, J. E. (2006). Qatar and the world: Branding for a micro-state. *The Middle East Journal, 60*(4), 732–748. https://doi.org/10.3751/60.4.15

Rookwood, J. (2019). Access, security and diplomacy: Perceptions of soft power, nation branding and the organizational challenges facing Qatar's 2022 FIFA World Cup. *Sport, Business and Management, 9*(1), 26–44.

Scharfenort, N. (2014). Off and running: Qatar brands for FIFA World Cup, and life beyond. In S. Wippel (Ed.), *Under construction* (pp. 71–87). Ashgate.

Schlumberger, O. (2010). Opening old bottles in search of new wine: On non-democratic legitimacy in the Middle East. *Middle East Critique, 19*(3), 233–250.

Sim, L.-C. (2012). Re-branding Abu Dhabi: From oil giant to energy titan. *Place Branding and Public Diplomacy, 8*(1), 83–98. https://doi.org/10.1057/pb.2011.31

The Business Year. (2013). Interview with Abdullah bin Hamad Al Attiyah. https://thebusinessyear.com/interview/important-sources/

The Denver Post. (2012, November 22). Qatar to host major climate talks. https://www.denverpost.com/2012/11/22/qatar-to-host-major-climate-talks/

Theodoropoulou, I., & Alos, J. (2020). Expect amazing! Branding Qatar as a sports tourism destination. *Visual Communication, 19*(1), 13–43. https://doi.org/10.1177/1470357218775005

Vuving, A. (2009). How soft power works. Paper presented at the panel "Soft Power and Smart Power," American Political Science Association annual meeting, Toronto. https://dkiapcss.edu/Publications/Vuving%20How%20soft%20power%20works%20APSA%202009.pdf

Windecker, G., & Sendrowicz, P. (2014). Qatar between marketing and realpolitik: A smart business model for a microstate? *KAS International Reports, 1.*

Wolfe, S. D. (2025). The hard edge of soft power: Mega-events, geopolitics, and making nations great again. In S. D. Wolfe (Ed.), *The hard edge of soft power.* Springer.

Zaabi, F. A., & Awamleh, R. (2019). Determinants of soft power: The case of The United Arab Emirates. In M. Stephens, M. El-Sholkamy, I. A. Moonesar, & R. Awamleh (Eds.), *Actions and insights—Middle East North Africa* (Vol. 7, pp. 57–74). Emerald Publishing Limited. https://doi.org/10.1108/S2048-757620190000007004

Zumbraegel, T. (2019). Being green or being seen green? Strategies of eco regime resilience in Qatar. In H. Pouran & H. Hakimian (Eds.), *Environmental challenges in the MENA region* (pp. 49–71). Gingko Library.

Zumbraegel, T. (2022). *Political power and environmental sustainability in Gulf monarchies*. Palgrave Macmillan.

Open Access This chapter is licensed under the terms of the Creative Commons Attribution 4.0 International License (http://creativecommons.org/licenses/by/4.0/), which permits use, sharing, adaptation, distribution and reproduction in any medium or format, as long as you give appropriate credit to the original author(s) and the source, provide a link to the Creative Commons license and indicate if changes were made.

The images or other third party material in this chapter are included in the chapter's Creative Commons license, unless indicated otherwise in a credit line to the material. If material is not included in the chapter's Creative Commons license and your intended use is not permitted by statutory regulation or exceeds the permitted use, you will need to obtain permission directly from the copyright holder.

CHAPTER 6

From "being there is everything" to "go big or go home"? Comparing the Opening Ceremonies of the 2008 Summer Olympics and the 2022 Winter Olympics in Beijing

Julia Gurol

Abstract This chapter discusses the rationales behind Chinese soft power projection by comparing the opening ceremonies of the 2008 Summer Olympics and the 2022 Winter Olympics. It shows that the Chinese party-state managed to instrumentalize both sporting events to its advantage by using the attention of millions at the opening ceremony to craft narratives of global development, to perform sleight of hand regarding international tensions, and to signal enhanced standing on the world stage.

Keywords Soft power • Authoritarianism • China • Opening ceremonies • Olympics

J. Gurol (✉)
German Institute for Global and Area Studies (GIGA), Hamburg, Germany
e-mail: julia.gurol-haller@giga-hamburg.de

© The Author(s) 2025
S. D. Wolfe (ed.), *The Hard Edge of Soft Power*, Mega Event Planning, https://Doi.org/10.1007/978-981-96-3515-3_6

INTRODUCTION

There is no democratic litmus test for hosts of (sporting) mega-events. In fact, that authoritarian countries seek to host mega-events is anything but new (Grix & Lee, 2013; Koch & Valiyev, 2015; Rookwood, 2022), as mega-events usually tend to serve their mega ambitions on the global stage. This chapter takes a closer look at the authoritarian country with the largest international mega ambitions, namely the People's Republic of China (PRC). When the Chinese party-state won the bid to host the 2008 Summer Olympics, critics pointed to the violation of human rights and social tensions existent in the country. At the same time, others noted the potential for improvement in these domains. Fourteen years later in 2022, reactions would be even more polarized as Beijing hosted the Winter Olympics in the context of the COVID-19 pandemic and increasingly tense international relations.

This raises a number of significant questions: to what exactly do mega-events offer a global stage, aside from the sport itself? Can this stage host questions of progressive activism and the possibility to highlight human rights violations, societal inequality, or the abuse of political power? Or does it offer the chance for the host country to cover up with glitter and glamor the skeletons hidden in the cupboard, providing a polished Potemkin image of itself to the watching world? While answers to these questions continue to divide scholars, a worthwhile point of focus is the PRC, as a country that has joined the club of host nations only rather recently. If hosting of sporting mega-events by authoritarian states like China polarizes observers to such a degree, and if the success of what is envisioned is so uncertain, what is it then that makes these countries willing to host mega-events over and over again? For the Chinese party-state, the answer here is undeniably "image management." Understanding mega-events as part of a nation's soft power toolbox, the attention, the glare of the international spotlight, and the emotions attached to global sport offered China the opportunity to reframe its image on the international stage (Cornelissen, 2010; Zheng et al., 2019).

While it has long been debated whether authoritarian states possess and actively project soft power, the Chinese case provides several instructive examples. By hosting mega-events like the 2008 Summer Olympics and 2022 Winter Olympics, China sought to show the world that it is the guardian of universal norms and, in so doing, can garner attention by illuminating truths such as "fair play" that are of universal appeal (Grix &

Lee, 2013; Lee, 2021). By allegedly guarding but in fact somewhat appropriating these universal norms, it can be said that the Chinese party-state somehow managed to present itself as a responsible global power, rightfully on the rise and promoting its traditional values. In this sense, the Chinese party-state successfully instrumentalized both mega-events to its advantage, capitalizing on the attention of millions at the opening ceremony to craft narratives of global development, to perform sleight of hand regarding international tensions, and to signal enhanced standing on the world stage.

This chapter discusses the rationales behind Chinese soft power projection, digging into the specificities of image management. By comparing the opening ceremonies of the 2008 Summer Olympics and the 2022 Winter Olympics, it further shows how deeply the instrumentalization of such sporting mega-events for reasons of soft power and public diplomacy is ingrained in the Chinese leadership's communication strategies. The choice to focus on the opening spectacles and not, for example, on the sporting events themselves stems from the proverbial "global stage" these ceremonies create for their host countries, and thus feed into their strong symbolic value (Adair, 2013). Not only are they the most widely watched television media events in the history of humankind (Tomlinson, 1996), they can also be understood as platforms that display universal humanistic messages, Olympic protocol and discourse, showcase nationhood, and combine global and local cultural content (Qing et al., 2010). When it comes to the opening ceremonies, no symbolism is too blunt, no spectacle too big, and no message too strong. The chapter concludes by discussing key aspects regarding the geopolitics of sporting mega-events more generally, and how authoritarian actors like China can use them for their own ends.

THE SPECIFICITIES OF CHINESE INTERNATIONAL POWER PROJECTION AND (AUTHORITARIAN) IMAGE MANAGEMENT

Regardless of whether we want to transfer the term "soft power" to authoritarian contexts or not, authoritarian state actors undeniably invest significant both intellectual and material resources in crafting and projecting a certain image of themselves and their regime to the world (Barr et al., 2015; Blanchard & Lu, 2012; Repnikova, 2022). Dukalskis (2021) coined this phenomenon "authoritarian image management." The latter is used to bind the domestic population more closely to the autocrat's rule, to create closer linkages in appealing to people's emotions and affections, and to strategically project a certain image to different audiences both at home and abroad. Be it the nostalgic longing for past times of blossoming and power or mythological promises of a better future woven into nationalist historical dreams (domestic audiences) or narratives of system supremacy and aspiring power claims (international audiences), certain symbols and narratives have become standard mechanisms of contemporary authoritarian regimes' toolboxes (Gurol, 2023; Klenk & Gurol, 2023). Recent literature on authoritarian regime survival has started to focus on what can be termed "authoritarian appeal"—namely the role of positive emotions, myths, or narratives for authoritarian stability, as examined via rhetoric, emotional appeals, and state responsiveness to the general public. For instance, in a study on party-people relations in China, Dickson argues that "some autocrats recognize that relying on coercion is costly and seek some semblance of popular support to maintain their rule" (Dickson, 2021). Hence the PRC can even be considered a frontrunner when it comes to image management, nation branding, and status signaling both domestically and on the world stage.

Before diving into the empirical evidence, it is first necessary to specify what roles are played by soft power projection in general and mega-event hosting in particular for the Chinese party-state. Over the past two decades, the Chinese Communist Party (CCP) has become increasingly active in seeking to influence political actors across the globe, while simultaneously rebranding the Chinese nation domestically (Gurol, 2023; Klenk & Gurol, 2023). In 2006, then-Chinese President Hu Jintao, predecessor to Xi Jinping, even declared the improving of China's soft power (软实力 *ruan shili*) to be one of the country's top foreign policy priorities, referring to forms such as media influence, propaganda, and cultural appeal. Since then, and internationally most visible following the official launch of the Belt and Road Initiative (BRI) in 2013, the CCP has used a multitude of methods to signal its aspired global status, to manage its image, and to "gain face" (要面子 *yao mianzi*) in the international arena (Pu, 2019).

Yao mianzi refers to a cultural understanding of respect, honor, and social standing that can easily be ascribed to Chinese international soft power endeavors. "Face" in this context refers to how one is viewed by others. In the Chinese understanding, it is something that can be earned and achieved (Buckley et al., 2006), for instance by hosting internationally glamorous sporting mega-events. A pivotal actor in these attempts to earn international prestige or to provide a model for emulation is the International Department of the Central Committee of the CCP (IDCCP), in particular as regards the Party's soft power initiatives targeting those living beyond the country's borders (Hackenesch & Bader, 2020). This is important especially in the context of the Chinese party-state's charm offensive toward countries and actors in the so-called Global South.

The Role of Sporting Mega-Events in China's Overall Image Management Strategy

Bidding for and hosting sporting mega-events seems, then, to be an ideal opportunity for the PRC to address both domestic and international audiences, thereby stirring patriotic sentiment among the Chinese public while simultaneously conveying national resurgence to the world (Chu, 2021). China has been hosting sporting mega-events since the 1990 Asian Games, held in Beijing, and will continue bidding for them in the future. For instance, as a next step, China is expected to plan an official bid to host the 2031 FIFA Women's World Cup, according to a plan issued jointly by the General Administration of Sport of China, Ministry of Education, Ministry of Finance, and the Chinese Football Association (CFA). Of particular importance though are the Olympics, as the event in the sporting calendar with the greatest social presence globally today and, alongside the FIFA Men's World Cup, boasting the most extensive reach worldwide (Close et al., 2007). The two iterations of this sporting mega-event that China has hosted so far, the 2008 Summer Olympics and the 2022 Winter Olympics, are now examined in more detail. The spectacles of their respective opening ceremonies are compared, thereby discussing these events' significance, symbolism, and overall messaging against the backdrop of China's broader image management strategy.

THE OPENING CEREMONIES OF THE 2008 SUMMER OLYMPICS AND THE 2022 WINTER OLYMPICS IN BEIJING

What a huge difference fourteen years can make. While in 2008 discussions around the Summer Olympics were infused with hopes for a liberalization of domestic politics and an improvement of human rights in China, the discourse in 2022—at least within the ranks of the International Olympic Committee (IOC)—was devoid of such positivity. On the contrary: learning from 2008, the IOC seemed now to sing a different tune, refraining from attaching any aspirations of political reform to the 2022 Games. While that silence might say much about the IOC as such, it also points to the geopolitics of such modern-day sporting mega-events. No longer do they provide a potential platform for progressive activism, but rather offer a means for authoritarian states like China to "sportswash" (Boykoff, 2022; Dooley, 2022; Dubinsky, 2023) their domestic politics and mask political tensions with glitter and glamor in the context of presenting a "spectacle" to the world (Koch, 2018). So what changed between 2008 and 2022? How can we understand the effects of both iterations of the Olympics in the context of China's broader image management endeavors over time? To answer these questions, the following sections dissect the rituals and symbols used in both opening ceremonies and thereby seek to draw conclusions regarding the Chinese party-state's political motives, interwoven into both of these spectacles.

First, when comparing the opening ceremonies that represent the prelude to the 2008 Summer Olympics and the 2022 Winter Olympics, it becomes clear that China hosted the latter with a marked increase in national self-awareness and self-confidence. The 2008 Games debuted China's new international stature and growing wealth. Moreover, they brought a high-profile global affirmation of the host regime's ongoing success in making the country "wealthy and strong" (*fuqiang* 富强), the raison d'être underpinning the activities of all Chinese nationalist leaders beginning with the country's humiliating nineteenth-century encounter with the West, through the early years of the PRC under Mao Zedong, into the reform and opening-up era of Deng Xiaoping, and continuing until Xi Jinping's currently third term in office. Accordingly, the 2008 opening ceremony combined elements of the local and the global, merging the country's cultural traditions and Confucian values with indicators of its new aspired-to status and opening up—that is, the culturally specific juxtaposed with the global commons (Chen et al., 2012; Economy & Segal, 2008).

The opening ceremony of the 2008 Summer Olympics was choreographed by Zhang Yimou, a famous Chinese filmmaker, who was hired by the CCP to create an extraordinary extravaganza portraying China's rich 5000-year-old history to the world. The spectacle would hence serve to illustrate the country's impressive cultural heritage to the international community (Elsborg, 2022), being a showcase example of soft power projection. It celebrated Chinese traditions and values and broadcast these around the globe. For instance, one part of the choreography consisted of

2800 drummers, beating a rhythm in unison on traditional bronze *fou* drums. Their choreography almost resembled a military parade, drawing up images of the purpose that stadiums served during communist and fascist times. At another point during the spectacle, scholars chanted Confucian Analects, yet another reference to traditional ancient Chinese values. The official slogan of the 2008 Summer Olympics underlined this endeavor: "One World, One Dream," signaling harmony and community while distracting from the country's domestic problems as well as tense international relations alike.

In terms of the domestic audience, according to Brady, the desire to host the Olympics and particularly the opening ceremony mainly served the purpose of "a propaganda campaign designed to mobilize the population around a common goal, and distract them from more troubling issues such as inflation, unemployment, political corruption and environmental degradation" (2009, n.p.), thereby creating unity and cohesion, and ultimately stability. A similar observation was made by Leibold (2010), who emphasized the acute tensions in Chinese society in the run-up to the 2008 Olympics that were supposed to be eased and/or covered up by this spectacle. For instance, in the run-up to the games, Chinese propaganda outlets pushed out preemptive narratives to counter against any potential criticism of the Party's "success" in hosting the Olympics. Despite the international attention drawn to the opening ceremonies, the domestic audience is of particular importance, as within the Chinese political system domestic politics generally trumps foreign policy. In other words, because of their direct link to the CCP's primary objective—regime survival—domestic issues take precedence over external ones. Pu offers a convincing argument for how the Chinese government wants to be received by different audiences: "Status signaling behaviors face a multiple audience problem, and for rising powers, the domestic audience is more important than the international audience" (Pu, 2019). In this sense, then, sporting spectacles provide the Chinese party-state the option to highlight Chinese values, power, and contributions, all while camouflaging underlying societal and political challenges.

Building on the 2008 legacy and having shown that the country had proved rather resilient to the criticism arising back then, the opening ceremony of the 2022 Winter Olympics—themed "Together for a Shared Future"—cast, in contrast, the image of a powerful and self-confident China now at play. The theme was also represented by the choreographies of the opening ceremony itself. In some ways, the opening ceremony and the Games themselves were overshadowed by the COVID-19 pandemic, being challenged by global restrictions on travel and beset by troubled international relations—in particular between the PRC and the United States, but also regarding Taiwan as well. Despite these challenges and increasing tensions, the CCP again used the extensive international attention paid to this spectacle to send a clear political message. In that regard, the symbols and images employed during the 2022 opening ceremony reflected clearly that China's international posture had shifted from adapting and merging the local and the global to now actively contesting established paradigms and seeking to set its own norms instead. For instance, each country delegation was accompanied by a Chinese representative, carrying a snowflake-shaped sign with the name of the delegation. Step by step, these snowflakes then gathered to form one large snowflake—a strong symbolism that the world is coming "together for a shared future," with China in the lead, mapping the way for the world to go.

In other words, it could be said that the two opening ceremonies reflect China's foreign policy shift from adaptation to contestation of pre-established norms and paradigms (Cabula & Pochettino, 2023). For a long time, China has followed the principle of *tao guang yang hui* (韬光养晦), which means "to calmly observe and maintain a low profile," coined by the former paramount leader of the country, Deng Xiaoping, in the early 1990s. In the context of China's opening policy and, most significantly, under Xi Jinping, it now follows the principle of *fen fa you wei* (奋发有为), which can be translated as "to actively strive for achievement" (Gurol, 2022; Yan, 2014). Although the opening ceremony offered in 2022 was not the same extravaganza and spectacle it had been fourteen years earlier, it delivered clear signals of geopolitical importance to domestic and international audiences alike. Orchestrated by Zhang Yimou once more, one of the big takeaways of the 2022 opening ceremony was China's self-depiction now as a technological superpower, with Beijing National Stadium's center stage being taken up by an enormous HD LED Screen (Elsborg, 2022). Interestingly, the technology used for the overall show is also the means by which the Chinese government has enhanced its authoritarian grip over and monitoring of its population, as showcased during the COVID-19 pandemic (Gurol et al., 2023; Gurol & Schütze, 2022). Similarly, the depiction of China's technological edge and innovative capabilities featured heavily in the CCP's "Made in China 2025" plan implemented since 2015, which seeks to make the country the frontrunner in global high-tech manufacturing. Hence, the 2022 opening ceremony can be read both as a celebration of previous achievements connected to China's global rise to power and as sending clear political signals regarding its future visions and aspirations as well.

Controversies and Criticism Around the Two Olympics Hosted by the Chinese Party-State

Both iterations of the Olympics hosted by the Chinese party-state attracted significant criticism from Western audiences, focused mostly on human rights violations and the situation in the country's Xinjiang province. In 2008, this even led some countries to declare a diplomatic boycott of the Games, meaning that no high-level officials would travel to Beijing to watch the show. In 2022 such criticism was even more pronounced, as based on the country's elevated global status and rising international tensions in the years between. According to Human Rights Watch (2022), 243 Nongovernmental Organizations (NGOs) from around the world criticized "atrocity crimes" and human rights violations by the Chinese government in the run-up to as well as during the course of the 2022 Winter Olympics. A further element was now added to the discussion here too: namely questions of sustainability and "green" sports, connected to sustainable legacies and discussions around authoritarian modernization (Horton & Saunders, 2012). Yet, in the case of the two Olympics hosted by the Chinese party-state, the latter played a significantly smaller role in the controversial discussions around the political and societal impact of the sporting mega-events.

Interestingly, despite the mounting criticism that came about during both iterations of the Olympics with this increasing global attention, the home front featured no significant policy changes nor challenges to the Chinese Communist Party's legitimacy. The party-state's image was no more tarnished due to hosting the Olympics than it had already been anyway. This calls into question the validity of claims that the hosting of sporting mega-events by authoritarian states can provide a platform for advocacy and (social or political) change by opening up new windows of opportunity for progressive activism and demonstration (see, e.g., Roche, 2017). Instead, they can cause or reinforce what John Horne calls and criticizes as a "routinization of harm to local populations" (Horne, 2018, p. 11). While the increased international attention usually leads to more vocal criticism by international actors of all kinds as well as different NGOs, the actual change their criticism causes is mostly rather minimal. On the contrary, the examples of the 2008 Summer Olympics and the 2022 Winter Olympics showed that what actually ultimately prevails here is a given host country having had the chance to present an image crafted entirely by its most important statespersons in order to display an idealized impression and understanding of itself to the world, while either hiding, "camouflaging" (Pauschinger, 2020), or even blatantly instrumentalizing international criticism to steer criticism in more favorable directions. One example of this tendency occurred in the 2022 opening ceremony, when Dinigeer Yilamujiang, a Uyghur[1] athlete, delivered the Olympic flame in Beijing. The choice to have a Uyghur cross-country skier light the torch is a clear example of sportswashing, particularly against the backdrop of China facing heavy scrutiny from international NGOs and governments alike over accusations of human rights violations and abuses against the Uyghur population, as well as in the light of increased international criticism regarding its foreign policy. Instrumentalizing the skier's Uyghur heritage in this highly nationalist spectacle can be interpreted not only as an aggressive retort to the criticism of China as Olympic host but also as a symbol of the party-state's nationalism and its program of forced assimilation, especially in regard to the overall idea that the Olympic Games should represent unity in both national and international contexts.

Conclusion

This chapter sheds light on the geopolitics of sporting mega-events in the context of China's broader image management strategy. Scrutinizing the opening ceremonies of the 2008 Summer Olympics and 2022 Winter Olympics, it revealed how the CCP made use on both occasions of the global stage provided by these mega-events to craft a spectacle carrying strong symbolism: namely of China as an aspiring global power. Not only was the CCP able to demonstrate its ability to host the world's most prestigious and high-profile events, but also to stir feelings of patriotism, convey national values, and share its cultural traditions. It is clear, then, that these spectacles serve a twin purpose in the context of soft power projection. On the one hand, they evidently address domestic audiences,

---

[1] Uyghurs are a predominantly Muslim Turkic ethnic group native to Xinjiang, China's most Western province.

boosting their nationalism, while seeking also to mask prevailing social tensions. On the other, they help project an image of power to international observers, not only showcasing China's rich culture and traditions but also sending a clear message in terms of the country's global aspirations.

Hence, the hosting of sporting mega-events by the Chinese Communist Party can be said to be driven by a mixture of national pride and political expediency—both oftentimes transformed into an enhanced grip over the Chinese population and serving the stability of the regime overall. The fact that the technology used during the 2022 opening ceremony is also used for surveillance shows the "hard edge" of soft power in authoritarian regimes and underlines the fact that the symbols, glitter, and glamor of the mega-event spectacles too often serve to camouflage actual policy mechanisms and lend authoritarian practices a soft and fluffy image. In general, it can be concluded that there is a fine line between image management, blatant soft power projection, and navigating the international criticism that typically becomes more pronounced in the run-up to these events. This highlights once more how sport is by no means apolitical, and that mega-events have indeed become a key element in geopolitics (Koch, 2018).[2] This also resonates with the message in this volume's introduction, and that is in fact repeated to some degree in every chapter here: "mega-events succeed at spectacle but at little else."

REFERENCES

Adair, D. (2013). Olympic ceremonial, protocol and symbolism. In S. Frawley & D. Adair (Eds.), *Managing the Olympics* (pp. 182–205). Palgrave Macmillan UK. https://doi.org/10.1057/9780230389588_11

Barr, M., Feklyunina, V., & Theys, S. (2015). Introduction: The soft power of hard states. *Politics, 35*(3–4), 213–215. https://doi.org/10.1111/1467-9256.12210

Blanchard, J.-M. F., & Lu, F. (2012). Thinking hard about soft power: A review and critique of the literature on China and soft power. *Asian Perspective, 36*(4), 565–589. https://doi.org/10.1353/apr.2012.0021

Boykoff, J. (2022). Toward a theory of sportswashing: Mega-events, soft power, and political conflict. *Sociology of Sport Journal, 39*(4), 342–351. https://doi.org/10.1123/ssj.2022-0095

---

[2] For further information on the bigger picture regarding the long-term implications of mega-events, see the related database and accompanying article by Müller et al. (2022).

Brady, A.-M. (2009). The Beijing Olympics as a campaign of mass distraction. *The China Quarterly, 197*, 1–24.

Buckley, P. J., Clegg, J., & Tan, H. (2006). Cultural awareness in knowledge transfer to China—The role of guanxi and mianzi. *Journal of World Business, 41*(3), 275–288. https://doi.org/10.1016/j.jwb.2006.01.008

Cabula, M., & Pochettino, S. (2023). Emerging negative soft power: The evolution of China's identity in the 2008 and 2022 Beijing Olympics opening and closing ceremonies. *The International Spectator, 58*(2), 17–34. https://doi.org/10.1080/03932729.2023.2195337

Chen, C. C., Colapinto, C., & Luo, Q. (2012). The 2008 Beijing Olympics opening ceremony: Visual insights into China's soft power. *Visual Studies, 27*(2), 188–195. https://doi.org/10.1080/1472586X.2012.677252

Chu, M. P. (2021). *China's quest for sporting mega-events: The politics of international bids*. Routledge.

Close, P., Askew, D., & Xu, X. (2007). *The Beijing Olympiad: The political economy of a sporting mega-event* (1. publ ed.). Routledge.

Cornelissen, S. (2010). The geopolitics of global aspiration: Sport mega-events and emerging powers. *The International Journal of the History of Sport, 27*(16–18), 3008–3025. https://doi.org/10.1080/09523367.2010.508306

Dickson, B. J. (2021). *The party and the people: Chinese politics in the 21st century*. Princeton University Press.

Dooley, B. (2022). *Sportswashing: The 2022 Beijing Olympics. 1 Oliver's Yard, 55 City Road, London EC1Y 1SP*. SAGE Publications: SAGE Business Cases Originals. https://doi.org/10.4135/9781529607987

Dubinsky, Y. (2023). Nation branding, public diplomacy, and the dirty business of sportswashing. In *Nation branding and sports diplomacy* (pp. 157–191). Springer International Publishing. https://doi.org/10.1007/978-3-031-32550-2_7

Dukalskis, A. (2021). *Making the world safe for dictatorship*. Oxford University Press.

Economy, E. C., & Segal, A. (2008). China's Olympic nightmare: What the games mean for Beijing's future. *Foreign Affairs, 87*(4), 47–56.

Elsborg, S. (2022, February 8). A modest but confident China on display at the 2022 Beijing Olympics opening ceremony. *Play the Game*. https://www.playthegame.org/news/a-modest-but-confident-china-on-display-at-the-2022-beijing-olympics-opening-ceremony/

Grix, J., & Lee, D. (2013). Soft power, sports mega-events and emerging states: The lure of the politics of attraction. *Global Society, 27*(4), 521–536. https://doi.org/10.1080/13600826.2013.827632

Gurol, J. (2022). *The EU-China security paradox: Cooperation against all odds?* Bristol University Press.

Gurol, J. (2023). The authoritarian narrator: China's power projection and its reception in the Gulf. *International Affairs, 99*(2), 687–705. https://doi.org/10.1093/ia/iiac266

Gurol, J., & Schütze, B. (2022). Infrastructuring authoritarian power: Arab-Chinese transregional collaboration beyond the state. *International Quarterly for Asian Studies, 53*(2), 231–249.

Gurol, J., Zumbrägel, T., & Demmelhuber, T. (2023). Elite networks and the transregional dimension of authoritarianism: Sino-Emirati relations in times of a global pandemic. *Journal of Contemporary China, 32*(139), 138–151. https://doi.org/10.1080/10670564.2022.2052444

Hackenesch, C., & Bader, J. (2020). The struggle for minds and influence: The Chinese Communist Party's global outreach. *International Studies Quarterly, 64*(3), 723–733. https://doi.org/10.1093/isq/sqaa028

Horne, J. (2018). Understanding the denial of abuses of human rights connected to sports mega-events. *Leisure Studies, 37*(1), 11–21. https://doi.org/10.1080/02614367.2017.1324512

Horton, P., & Saunders, J. (2012). The 'East Asian' Olympic Games: What of sustainable legacies? *The International Journal of the History of Sport, 29*(6), 887–911. https://doi.org/10.1080/09523367.2011.617587

Human Rights Watch. (2022). Beijing Olympics begin amid atrocity crimes. https://www.hrw.org/news/2022/01/27/beijing-olympics-begin-amid-atrocity-crimes

Klenk, E., & Gurol, J. (2023). The role of narratives for gaining domestic political legitimacy: China's image management during COVID-19. *Journal of Chinese Political Science.* https://doi.org/10.1007/s11366-023-09865-z

Koch, N. (2018). *The geopolitics of spectacle: Space, synecdoche, and the new capitals of Asia.* Cornell University Press.

Koch, N., & Valiyev, A. (2015). Urban boosterism in closed contexts: Spectacular urbanization and second-tier mega-events in three Caspian capitals. *Eurasian Geography and Economics, 56*(5), 575–598. https://doi.org/10.1080/15387216.2016.1146621

Lee, J. W. (2021). Olympic Winter Games in non-Western Cities: State, sport and cultural diplomacy in Sochi 2014, PyeongChang 2018 and Beijing 2022. *The International Journal of the History of Sport, 38*(13–14), 1494–1515. https://doi.org/10.1080/09523367.2021.1973441

Leibold, J. (2010). The Beijing Olympics and China's conflicted national form. *The China Journal, 63*, 1–24.

Müller, M., Wolfe, S. D., Gogishvili, D., Gaffney, C., Hug, M., & Leick, A. (2022). The mega-events database: Systematising the evidence on mega-event outcomes. *Leisure Studies, 41*(3), 437–445. https://doi.org/10.1080/02614367.2021.1998835

Pauschinger, D. (2020). The permeable Olympic fortress: Mega-event security as camouflage in Rio de Janeiro. *Conflict and Society, 6*(1), 108–127. https://doi.org/10.3167/arcs.2020.060107

Pu, X. (2019). *Rebranding China: Contested status signaling in the changing global order*. Stanford University Press.

Qing, L., Boccia, V. L., Chunmiao, H., Xing, L., Fu, Y., & Kennett, C. (2010). Representing the opening ceremony: Comparative content analysis from USA, Brazil, UK and China. *The International Journal of the History of Sport, 27*(9–10), 1591–1633. https://doi.org/10.1080/09523367.2010.481115

Repnikova, M. (2022). *Chinese soft power* (1st ed.). Cambridge University Press. https://doi.org/10.1017/9781108874700

Roche, M. (2017). *Mega-events and social change: Spectacle, legacy and public culture*. Manchester University Press. https://doi.org/10.7765/9781526117090

Rookwood, J. (2022). From sport-for-development to sports mega-events: Conflict, authoritarian modernisation and statecraft in Azerbaijan. *Sport in Society, 25*(4), 847–866. https://doi.org/10.1080/17430437.2021.2019710

Tomlinson, A. (1996). Olympic spectacle: Opening ceremonies and some paradoxes of globalization. *Media, Culture & Society, 18*(4), 583–602. https://doi.org/10.1177/016344396018004005

Yan, X. (2014). From keeping a low profile to striving for achievement. *The Chinese Journal of International Politics, 7*(2), 153–184. https://doi.org/10.1093/cjip/pou027

Zheng, J., Chen, S., Tan, T.-C., & Houlihan, B. (Eds.). (2019). *Sport policy in China*. Routledge/Taylor & Francis Group.

Open Access This chapter is licensed under the terms of the Creative Commons Attribution 4.0 International License (http://creativecommons.org/licenses/by/4.0/), which permits use, sharing, adaptation, distribution and reproduction in any medium or format, as long as you give appropriate credit to the original author(s) and the source, provide a link to the Creative Commons license and indicate if changes were made.

The images or other third party material in this chapter are included in the chapter's Creative Commons license, unless indicated otherwise in a credit line to the material. If material is not included in the chapter's Creative Commons license and your intended use is not permitted by statutory regulation or exceeds the permitted use, you will need to obtain permission directly from the copyright holder.

CHAPTER 7

The Authoritarian Legacy: Mega-Event Security, the Managerial-Militarized Model, and the Rise of the Far-Right in Brazil

Bruno Cardoso and Dennis Pauschinger

Abstract Only two years after the 2016 Olympics closed in Rio de Janeiro's Maracanã stadium, far-right candidate Jair Bolsonaro won the national elections with a campaign rooted in authoritarian and hateful discourse against minorities and praising the nation's military past. Much has been written about the roots of Bolsonaro's success and his strong support in the Brazilian security apparatus. This chapter brings a new angle to this discussion and argues that the ways in which the security schemes for Brazil's mega-event decade were organized laid the ground for a successful Bolsonaro campaign and government. In the years prior to the 2014 World Cup, the Brazilian state implemented an integrated command and control system to develop a managerial-militarized model for organizing public security and the technological system built for the mega-events. The chapter explores how this approach enforced a military urbanism, a

B. Cardoso
Federal University of Rio de Janeiro, Rio de Janeiro, Brazil

D. Pauschinger (✉)
University of Neuchâtel, Biel, Switzerland

© The Author(s) 2025
S. D. Wolfe (ed.), *The Hard Edge of Soft Power*, Mega Event Planning, https://doi.org/10.1007/978-981-96-3515-3_7

New Public Management, and benchmarking strategies that still mark Brazil's public security sector. It argues that the heavy influence of military strategies intermingled with new neoliberal economic thinking that laid the ground for a successful authoritarian candidate like Bolsonaro who based his government upon these exact values.

Keywords Authoritarianism • Securitization • Brazil • Olympics • Football World Cup

Introduction: Hosting Mega-Events

Brazil hosted the world's two most prestigious events in a single decade. Despite protests and public resistance to how mega-events have been organized, the prestige of hosting is still desirable for city governors and country leaders. Mayors see the possibility of hosting mega-events as a means to hype up their city's marketing, and investors see the opportunity for good deals (Ward, 2007; Gold & Gold, 2017, 10). Mega-events serve equally as geopolitical projects for national leaders to reaffirm their aspiration to power (Cornelissen, 2010; Wolfe, 2020). Such soft power aspirations were not different in Brazil, where the national government wanted mega-events as a means to position the country among major nations. At the same time, local politicians in Rio thought of hosting as an opportunity to boost the city as a tourist hotspot and to achieve this through improving the long-standing urban conflict between the police, drug trafficking organizations, and militias.

In recent years, mega-events have been associated with countries where authoritarian leaders and state structures are predominant. Authoritarianism seems to be a fertilizer to host in relative peace from activists and local political uprising. On the foundation of this book's approach to authoritarian practices, we explore how mega-events can lay the ground for developments that favor the rise of the far-right. In this light, mega-events can be seen as linked to a rise of authoritarian politicians and politics that threaten democracies on a global scale. There is no more illustrative example than the mega-event decade in Brazil with the 2014 World Cup and the 2016 Rio Olympics.[1]

---

[1] Brazil also hosted other mega-events, from the Pan American Games in 2007 to the Paralympic Games in 2016, as well as the FIFA Confederations Cup in 2013.

These mega-events were awarded to Brazil when President Lula da Silva from the Workers' Party was in power. A skyrocketing economy seemed to lift the notorious "country of the future"[2] out of the shadows of its economically troubled and militaristic past. Millions were pulled out of poverty and brought the country closer to mitigating the social divisions dating to the times of slavery. The World Cup and the Olympics were meant to be the pinnacles of the country's success. Eight years after the end of the 2016 Olympics, next to nothing is left of this enthusiasm.

To the contrary, just before the Olympics, President Dilma Rousseff was impeached on flawed allegations of financial irresponsibility, a major setback for the country's democratic values (Rocha, 2019) and a turning point in the political crisis for the country. In 2018, Lula was imprisoned as part of this process, based on at least highly questionable evidence (Carvalho & Fonseca, 2019). Rio de Janeiro State declared a state of financial emergency, the former Governor Sérgio Cabral was jailed over World Cup construction contracts (Mazieiro, 2018), and the country still fights with recession and skyrocketing levels of violence and unemployment (Hirata et al., 2023).

Brazil has not been immune to the global trend that brought extreme right-wing politicians to power. The political polarization after Rousseff's impeachment and Lula's imprisonment, mixed with a wave of disinformation, elected extreme right-wing populist Jair Bolsonaro as president in 2018. In the State of Rio, Wilson Witzel rode the same political wave but faced a rapid removal from the governor's office. Notably, his attention-grabbing proposal to combat drug traffickers involved deploying elite police snipers, overshadowing substantive plans for addressing political and economic issues. Witzel's successor in office, Governor Cláudio Castro, similarly relies on the politics of violence.

Bolsonaro, with decades of experience in Congress, presented himself and his party as the "new" politics, free from corruption and with easy solutions for public security issues. Yet, he and his family are tied to racist (Phillips, 2020a), homophobic (Sullivan, 2018), and sexist (Euronews, 2019) commentary and have links to Rio's most violent militias (Pougy & Greenwald, 2019). As president, Bolsonaro made world news with his inaction and denial of the gravity of the COVID-19 pandemic, ridiculing

---

[2] Stefan Zweig wrote "Brazil, country of the future" (1942) while in exile in the country. Since then, this title has become a national emblem, a symbol of hope and, at times, a criticism of missed opportunities.

the death of thousands (Farzan & Berger, 2020; Phillips, 2020b). Moreover, he appointed military personnel to political office, incentivized political violence, and threatened not to recognize election results in his attempt for a second term (Biller & Bridi, 2022). After he lost the 2022 elections against Lula, who ran to restore his political legacy, Bolsonaro stayed silent for days while his loyalists planned terrorist attacks (Folha de S. Paulo, 2023). On January 8, 2023, pro-Bolsonaro protesters stormed the national congress, the governmental palace, and the federal Supreme Court buildings in Brasília (Jeantet & Biller, 2023).

We argue the organization of mega-event security laid the ground for a successful Bolsonaro campaign and later government. Hosting mega-events means that local governments must follow standardized security measures based upon the employment of military forces, cutting-edge surveillance technologies, and the transformation of public space into public-private enclaves of security spectacles. Unlike previous events, the main security focus for the events was not terrorism but the ongoing urban conflict in Rio de Janeiro. Involving police, political actors, and drug trafficking groups, the conflict leads to frequent shootouts and casualties across different neighborhoods. Security was a key issue that had to be solved for the World Cup and the Olympics.

One year before the World Cup, the Brazilian state implemented an integrated command and control system to develop a managerial-militarized model of thinking and organizing public safety through a technological system built for the mega-events in Rio. Within this system, national, regional, and local Integrated Command and Control Centers (CICC)[3] were built as a strategy to produce and stabilize relations between agents and institutions. The influence of military strategies, a security technologies infrastructure, and new neoliberal economic thinking all lay the ground for a successful authoritarian candidate like Bolsonaro. In this chapter we analyze (1) how mega-event security architecture was created in Rio de Janeiro; (2) how a managerial system was brought together with

[3] SICC—Integrated Command and Control System, composed of 13 Integrated Command and Control Centers (CICCs), one in each World Cup host city, as well as a national one in Brasilia. Managed by the Ministry of Justice, the SICC operates the connection and centralization of operations, as well as a national security strategy. The CICCs are centralized socio-technical infrastructures, where agents from different security forces work together. The CICC-RJ is the largest, located in Rio de Janeiro and commanded by the Rio de Janeiro Military Police, with the presence of agents from other security forces. Much of the fieldwork and interviews for this chapter were carried out in the CICC-RJ.

traditional oppressive policing; (3) the increase of State militarization in Brazil after the mega-events; and (4) how this system played an essential role for the authoritarian movement of Bolsonaro.

The Brazilian Mega-Event Security System

The mega-event preparations brutally transformed Rio de Janeiro's urban landscape, deepening the racialized socio-spatial divisions through favela evictions and resettlements of poor populations to guarantee event security (Talbot, 2024). Another strategy was the implementation of the Pacifying Police Unit (UPP), a militarized security strategy to install permanent Military Police units in 38 favelas that were important for the mega-events (Richmond, 2019). The other security strategies that were more explicitly linked to the mega-events can be coalesced into three simplified pillars: (1) the integration of the many different security agencies involved in mega-event security planning; (2) technological surveillance and communication strategies; and (3) militarized policing (Pauschinger, 2020a, 2020b).

For the first pillar, the Brazilian government implemented the Integrated Command and Control System (SICC), bringing together the Ministries of Justice and Defense, police institutions, the military, and the intelligence agencies—in short, everything involved with mega-event security. To materialize this strategy, Brazilian authorities founded the Extraordinary Secretariat for Mega-Event Security (SESGE).

The second pillar comprised infrastructures that supported the SICC, achieved by constructing Integrated Command and Control Centers (CICCs) from which mega-event security operations were coordinated (Cardoso, 2013). Aside from one main center, there were also mobile CICC trucks around the sport venues during the mega-events.

The third pillar—militarized policing strategies—is most relevant here. The policing strategies at the World Cup and the Olympics differed in some details, but the policing model was a merger between traditional policing strategies in Rio de Janeiro and what is well known from the globalized standards of mega-event security: green zone strategies (Chandrasekaran, 2000; Mowle, 2007), isolating urban areas around sport venues to produce security islands with checkpoints, metal detectors, and a plethora of state and private security employees (e.g., Fussey & Klauser, 2015).

Policing the rest of the city was undertaken by the Federal, Military, and Civil Police, the National Public Security Force, the Armed Forces, and the Municipal Guards. Overall, the Olympics featured 88,000 security agents, including 41,000 military personnel (SECOM, 2016: 4). Different police institutions patrolled relevant neighborhoods in tandem with the Armed Forces, and Rio was transformed for some weeks into a spectacular militarized security fortress.

COMMAND, CONTROL, AND THE PARADIGM SHIFT

The combination of neoliberalism and militarism is nothing new in South America,[4] and has never seemed to bother the proponents of neoliberal economics (Dardot & Laval, 2014). In the Brazilian case, however, this combination occurred through a specific model of public management, called "managerial-militarized" logic by Cardoso (2019a), which connects the authoritarian and violent tradition of the local armed forces with simplified conceptions of management, enrolled through the technological infrastructure of the SICC.

The official discourse of the government was that mega-event security preparations would leave two major legacies in Rio de Janeiro, one material—the technological infrastructure acquired for the mega-events and which make up the SICC—and the other immaterial, a "paradigm shift" to the security forces. In addition to integrating different agencies and institutions into a network model, the paradigm shift was related to the use of information technologies to increase the efficiency of security policies and actions. Managers promised a more intelligent security policy, less associated with violence and corruption, working with good practices of new public management (Dardot & Laval, 2014), and with crime prediction capabilities through data analysis (Garland, 2001; Cardoso, 2013; Cardoso & Hirata, 2017; Duarte, 2019).

Promising that technology would transform the way the state operates, the government also considered the companies that offered software, hardware, and support for this infrastructure. The security technology industry plays an important role not only in defining what security means (Leander, 2005) but also in the very way the state operates (Cardoso, 2018). When companies design ICT systems, they also build action

---

[4] The dictatorships of Augusto Pinochet in Chile (1973–1988) and Alberto Fujimori in Peru (1992–2000) are paradigmatic examples.

programs (Latour, 1992) that organize objectives and how these objectives are pursued. In this, a neoliberal normativity is invisibly incorporated into software, georeferenced maps, and metadata (Badouard et al., 2016). Moreover, the officers who were assigned to manage the CICC had completed MBAs in administration, offered by agreement between a prestigious Brazilian public school (EBAPE-FGV) and the state security department. The creation of this socio-technical system was an auxiliary strategy in the implementation of neoliberal norms that were supposed to restructure the Brazilian state.

The logic of corporate management of the state and neoliberal normativity took on their own contours and led to specific configurations when applied to the complexities of public security. A first obstacle to coordinating/integrating action was the fragmented structure of public security in the country, composed of various agencies at national, state, and municipal levels. Fragmentation entails issues such as the creation of separate databases, which are often unknown to each other or do not communicate, the carrying out of redundant tasks, the "damming up" of valuable information, and institutional dispute over attributions, resources, and recognition.

Governments promised that the SICC paradigm shift would be radical and efficient, building a reality against which dissatisfied agents and institutions could not fight. This complex composition of architecture, documents, business management principles, people, and communication technologies would result in operational coordination and information integration. The effects obtained would be the organization and stabilization of relations between individuals and institutions in a more rationalized and efficient form, through a command and control model. Mega-event hosting brought an urgency that accelerated this unprecedented national articulation in public security. The modernization of the country as a result of hosting mega-events took place in many different ways.

Command and control is a military doctrine and organizational principle (Walker et al., 2017). In Brazil, it was initially adopted by the Ministry of Defense and the Armed Forces by decree. Subsequently, some state security departments also adopted it as a normative model. In simplified terms, it advocates a well-defined command and obedience structure, characterized by its constitution in a network that can assimilate other networks or recompose itself indefinitely, varying the center and changing the chain of action according to the situation. Implementing the command and control model nationally requires overlapping security organization at state and federal levels.

The rationalized placement of people was said to produce coordinated action and quality social relationships. According to managers interviewed by Cardoso (2013) and Pauschinger (2024), the personal relations between representatives from different agencies sharing the same space would encourage collaboration. Pauschinger (2024) evaluates this strategy based on the reflections of those who made up the CICC during the mega-events. Physically occupying the same place, under intense conditions in a period of maximum programmed exceptionality, was not successful in producing later coordinated action. As emphasized in interviews with CICC participants during the World Cup, the exceptional characteristics that shaped the mega-event period were not representative of the conditions of everyday action, nor were they easily reproducible on a day-to-day basis (Pauschinger, 2024).

In practice, a decade after the system was inaugurated, public security in Rio de Janeiro has not seen positive developments. During this time, CICC managers in Rio de Janeiro applied benchmarking strategies to the police officers who work there (Cardoso, 2019b), created protocols for individual and inter-agency action, and referenced doctrines to serve as the basis for the center's operation. The most notable effects were the strengthening of the managerial-militarized model (Cardoso, 2019a) and the rise of the extreme right in Brazil.

Continuities of the Past: Militarization and the Rise of the Far-Right

Since its inauguration in 2013, the CICC has played an increasingly prominent role in Rio management. Whether during mega-events, demonstrations and protests, or in police raids to invade or occupy favelas, operations were always planned and monitored from this building. In each situation, the security forces used large-scale warfare and strategies inspired by war operations. The centrality of the SICC in the planning and execution of security operations consolidated through authoritarian practices an increasingly militarized approach to security issues.

Security operations during the mega-events are examples of the spectacular effects produced by the mobilization and coordination of this socio-technical network, operated by different agencies. The security forces used helicopters to accompany demonstrations or delegations, multiplied physical barriers to channel flows of pedestrians or vehicles, mobilized contingents of heavily armed security agents, cordoned off security perimeters, and made extensive use of low-lethality weapons.

During the mega-events, the security plan was to build a "fortress" (Pauschinger, 2020b) that encompassed all areas of interest, such as tourist spots, competition spaces, and the traveling routes for spectators and delegations. These strategies were learned, developed, and put into operation throughout the entire mega-event cycle. The major demonstrations that took place in Brazil during the Confederations Cup in June 2013 had repercussions on the preparation for the 2014 World Cup and the 2016 Olympics. On these occasions, the security forces set up green zones, monitored social networks, used undercover agents in protesters' organizations, and preventively arrested 23 activists on the eve of the World Cup final. The know-how to shut down protests and demonstrations was an important security legacy of these events. Scenes of violent protests would not be repeated until 2023, when Bolsonaro supporters invaded the seats of power in Brasilia. According to subsequent investigations, it was the deliberate negligence of the capital's Military Police that allowed the protesters to attack government buildings, rather than their inability to handle the situation (Caldas, 2024).

One element that exacerbates the effects of the militarization of security is the already high lethality rate in Rio de Janeiro's police actions. The violence and authoritarian practices that structure relations between the security forces and the population are much higher than in most cities without a declared state of war. We see in Rio de Janeiro a new military urbanism (Graham, 2010), leading to a considerable increase in homicide rates and police violence since the CICC began operation. During the mega-event period from 2013 to 2016, intentional violent deaths went from 32.7 to 37.6 per 100,000 inhabitants, while deaths resulting from police action increased from 2.6 to 5.6 per 100,000 (Forum Brasileiro de Segurança Pública, 2024). Although it is not possible to link this increase to the functioning of the CICC, its predicted positive effects were not felt in homicide and police violence rates.

In 2018, an election year in Brazil, then-President Michel Temer decreed a federal intervention in Rio de Janeiro on the grounds of the state's fiscal and security crisis. In practice, it was an army intervention. The CICC became the headquarters of the military leadership, which then managed a substantial part of the state, commanding the police and intelligence apparatus, as well as important material resources and a substantial portion of the state budget.

The appointed intervention cabinet was made up of five generals, a colonel, and a police chief. They dealt with a Rio de Janeiro plagued by the economic and political crisis that followed the mega-events (Hirata et al., 2023), with insubordinate police forces and overdue salaries, and the state governor under investigation for corruption.[5] For 10 months, General Braga Netto became the most important political figure in the state. There followed serious violations of fundamental freedoms, attacks on the lives of favela residents (Leite, 2000, 2012), and authoritarian practices as a technology of government (Fernandes, 2020).

The federal intervention in Rio de Janeiro in 2018 was important, but much more followed. To the surprise of most political analysts, two candidates from small parties who ran relatively modest campaigns with extreme right-wing platforms were elected Rio de Janeiro governor and president of Brazil. Wilson Witzel, now governor, was a federal judge, while President-elect Jair Bolsonaro was an army officer and then an obscure parliamentarian. Both explicitly promised a security policy based on increased police lethality and the extermination of *vagabundos*,[6] with inflammatory speeches of "law and order."

Bolsonaro's government (2019–2022) was the pinnacle of militarized managerialism (Nozaki, 2021). The number of military personnel appointed to important positions in the Brazilian state apparatus peaked, with a higher number of military ministers than during the military dictatorship (1964–1985). However, Bolsonaro's election is itself a consequence of the process of militarization of the state, based on a managerial-militarized logic, which has mega-events as one of its roots. The best example of this process is the paradigmatic trajectory of General Braga Netto. In less than ten years, he was General Coordinator of the Special Advisory Body for the Rio 2016 Olympic and Paralympic Games (2013–2016), Intervenor in Rio de Janeiro (2018) and, in the Bolsonaro government, Chief of Staff (2019), coordinator of the "Crisis Committee for Supervision and Monitoring of the Impacts of Covid-19" (2020),

---

[5] Governor Luiz Pezão was arrested on November 29, 2018, a month before the end of his term.

[6] Something like "tramp" or "vagabond" in English, which in local slang mixes the idea of not working with involvement in crime, often extending to behaviors associated with favela dwellers, mostly black and poor.

Secretary of State for Defense (2021), and vice-presidential candidate in Bolsonaro's failed re-election attempt (2022). From playing a major role in the security of the mega-events to the core of political life and institutional power in the country, Braga Netto's rapid rise in the state structure is not justified by the mediocre results he achieved, whether in the intervention in Rio de Janeiro, in the fight against Covid, or in coordinating the Bolsonaro government.

Conclusion

The aftermath of the Olympics witnessed an escalation in state violence. A scene much referenced (Pauschinger, 2023, 2024; Fernandes, 2020) is Rio de Janeiro's far-right Governor Witzel filmed three years after the Olympics, descending from a helicopter on the Rio-Niterói Bridge, running toward the sniper who had killed a hijacker (in an operation led by the CICC), cheering as if he had just scored the winning goal. During his time in office, Witzel actively encouraged police forces to shoot, which in 2019 led to 1810 people being killed by state forces—the highest number since measurements began in 1998, with a staggering rate of 11.4 deaths per 100,000 inhabitants (BBC, 2020). The composition of the spectacular performance and the discursive encouragement of killing, authorizing death and deciding who deserves to die, best illustrate how new benchmark security approaches are working with old traditions of oppressive policing. In contemporary Rio, security is exercised as necropolitics, in which killing becomes a form of security governance (Mbembe, 2006; Medeiros, 2018).

At the national level, the central mega-event legacy in terms of security was the consolidation of a managerial-militarized model that was, to a certain extent, a paradigm shift. Only to a certain extent, because the militarization of the state is nothing new in Brazil, a country in which 10 of the 34 presidents were military, and army influence on politics has been felt since the imperial period in the nineteenth century. However, this time the military were presented not only as "guarantors of order" but also as the most suitable managers to run the state apparatus. They presented themselves as technicians, not inclined to politics and averse to corruption, and were supported by the global conservative wave and the political crisis that followed Dilma Rousseff's impeachment and Lula's imprisonment.

The catastrophic Bolsonaro administration cannot be dissociated from the military that filled the state during this period. In 2020, members or former members of the Armed Forces occupied 10 ministries and 6157 civilian positions in the federal government, compared to 1427 in 2010, before the mega-events (Nozaki, 2021). However, the recent decline in the prestige of the military and the number of positions in the federal government does not mean the demilitarization of the state. Sociotechnical infrastructures such as the SICC reinforce modes of planning and action that reproduce authoritarian methods of spatial and population control, gradually normalizing them: an authoritarian legacy from the mega-events that will last for many years.

References

Badouard, R., Mabi, C., & Sire, G. (2016). Beyond "Points of Control": Logics of digital governmentality. *Internet Policy Review*, 5(3), 1–13.

BBC. (2020, January 23). Five people a day killed by Rio police in 2019. *BBC News*. Retrieved April 2, 2020, from https://www.bbc.com/news/world-latin-america-51220364

Biller, D., & Bridi, C. (2022). Bolsonaro contests Brazil election results, demands votes be anulled. *PBS NewsHour*. Retrieved March 23, 2024, from https://www.pbs.org/newshour/world/bolsonaro-contests-brazil-election-results-demands-votes-be-anulled

Caldas, A. L. (2024). PMDF indicia policiais em atos de 8/1; major preso è convocado pela CPI. *Agência Brasil*. Retrieved August 13, 2024, from https://agenciabrasil.ebc.com.br/radioagencia-nacional/justica/audio/2024-02/stf-forma-maioria-para-condenar-oficiais-da-pmdf-pelo-8-de-janeiro

Cardoso, B. (2013). Megaeventos esportivos e modernização tecnológica: planos e discursos sobre o legado em segurança pública [Sporting mega-events and technological modernisation: Plans and discourses on the legacy of public security]. *Horizontes Antropológicos*, 19(40), 119–148. https://doi.org/10.1590/S0104-71832013000200005

Cardoso, B. (2018). Estado, tecnologias de segurança e normatividade neoliberal [State, security technologies and neoliberal normativity]. In F. Bruno, B. Cardoso, M. Kanashiro, L. Guilhon, & L. Melgaço (Eds.), *Tecnopolíticas da vigilância: perspectivas da margem [Technopolitics of surveillance: Perspectives from the margin]*. São Paulo.

Cardoso, B. (2019a). A lógica gerencial-militarizada e a segurança pública no Rio de Janeiro: O CICC-RJ e as tecnologias de (re)construção do Estado [The managerial-militarized logic and public security in Rio de Janeiro: The CICC-RJ and the technologies of state (re)construction]. *Dilemas, Revista de Estudos de Conflito, Controle Social e Violência, Edição Especial*, 3, 53–74.

Cardoso, B. (2019b). Benchmarking et sècuritè à Rio de Janeiro. *Statistique et Sociètè, 7*(1), 25–30.
Cardoso, B., & Hirata, D. (2017). Dispositivos de inscrição e redes de ordenamento público: Uma aproximação entre a Teoria do Ator-Rede (ANT) e Foucault [Inscription devices and public ordering networks: An approach between Actor-Network Theory (ANT) and Foucault]. *Sociologia & Antropologia, 7*, 77–103.
Carvalho, C. A., & Fonseca, M. G. C. (2019). Violência em acontecimentos políticos: jornalismo e lawfare no caso Lula [Violence in political events: Journalism and lawfare in the Lula case]. *Galáxia (São Paulo), spe1*, 100–112. https://doi.org/10.1590/1982-25542019441720
Cerqueira, D., & Bueno, S. (eds.). (2024). Atlas da violência 2024. Brasília: Ipea; FBSP. Available at https://repositorio.ipea.gov.br/handle/11058/14031
Chandrasekaran, R. (2000). *Imperial life in the emerald city*. Bloomsbury Publishing.
Cornelissen, S. (2010). The geopolitics of global aspiration: Sport mega-events and emerging powers. *The International Journal of the History of Sport, 27*(16–18), 3008–3025. https://doi.org/10.1080/09523367.2010.508306
Dardot, P., & Laval, C. (2014). *The new way of the world: On neoliberal society*. Verso Books.
Duarte, D. E. (2019). *Reassembling security technologies* (Politics and international studies). King's College London .
Euronews. (2019). Brazil's Bolsonaro attacks Macron's wife in 'sexist' Facebook post. *Euronews*. Retrieved March 23, 2024, from https://www.euronews.com/2019/08/26/brazil-s-jair-bolsonaro-attacks-macron-s-wife-in-sexist-facebook-post
Farzan, A. N., & Berger, M. (2020). Bolsonaro says Brazilians must not be 'sissies' about coronavirus, as 'all of us are going to die one day'. *Washington Post*. Retrieved March 23, 2024, from https://www.washingtonpost.com/world/2020/11/11/bolsonaro-coronavirus-brazil-quotes/
Fernandes, C. T. (2020). "O rio da secura deságua na guerra": Integração, comando, controle e intervenção militar no Rio de Janeiro contemporâneo ["The river of dryness flows into war": Integration, command, control and military intervention in contemporary Rio de Janeiro]. *Revista de Estudos Empíricos em Direito, 7*(2), 180–202. https://doi.org/10.19092/reed.v7i2.465
Folha de S. Paulo. (2023). Bolsonarists convicted of bombing truck near airport in Brasilia. *Folha de S.Paulo*. Retrieved March 23, 2024, from https://www1.folha.uol.com.br/internacional/en/brazil/2023/05/bolsonarists-convicted-of-bombing-truck-near-airport-in-brasilia.shtml
Fussey, P., & Klauser, F. (2015). Securitisation and the mega-event: An editorial introduction. *The Geographical Journal, 181*(3), 194–198.

Garland, D. (2001). *The culture of control: Crime and social order in contemporary society* (Vol. 77). Oxford University Press. Retrieved March 6, 2024.

Gold, J. R., & Gold, M. M. (2017). Introduction. In J. R. Gold & M. M. Gold (Eds.), *Olympic cities: City agendas, planning, and the world's games, 1896–2020* (3rd ed., pp. 1–17). Routledge.

Graham, S. (2010). *Cities under siege: The new military urbanism.* Verso.

Hirata, D. V., Grillo, C. C., & Telles, V. D. S. (2023). Guerra urbana e expansão de mercados no Rio de Janeiro. *Revista Brasileira de Ciências Sociais, 38*(111), e3811003. https://doi.org/10.1590/3811003/2023

Jeantet, D., & Biller, D. (2023). Pro-Bolsonaro rioters storm Brazil's top government offices. *AP News.* Retrieved March 23, 2024, from https://apnews.com/article/jair-bolsonaro-brazil-government-caribbean-0c03c098a5e2a09ac534412c30ae8355

Latour, B. (1992). Where are the missing masses? The sociology of a few mundane artifacts. *Shaping technology/building society: Studies in sociotechnical change, 1,* 225–258.

Leander, A. (2005). The power to construct international security: On the significance of private military companies. *Millennium: Journal of International Studies, 33*(3), 803–825. https://doi.org/10.1177/03058298050330030601

Leite, M. P. (2000). Entre o individualismo e a solidariedade: dilemas da política e da cidadania no Rio de Janeiro [Between individualism and solidarity: Dilemmas of politics and citizenship in Rio de Janeiro]. *Revista Brasileira de Ciências Sociais, 15*(44), 73–90. https://doi.org/10.1590/S0102-69092000000300004

Leite, M. P. (2012). Da "metáfora da guerra" ao projeto de "pacificação": favelas e políticas de segurança pública no Rio de Janeiro [From the "metaphor of war" to the project of "pacification": Favelas and public security policies in Rio de Janeiro]. *Revista Brasileira de Segurança Pública, 6*(2), 374–388. https://doi.org/10.31060/rbsp.2012.v6.n2.126

Mazieiro, G. (2018). Cabral è condenado a 12 anos de prisão por superfaturamento no Maracanã e PAC Favelas [Cabral is sentenced to 12 years in prison for overbilling at Maracanã and PAC Favelas]. Retrieved March 23, 2024, from https://noticias.uol.com.br/politica/ultimas-noticias/2018/09/12/cabral-e-condenado-a-por-obras-do-maracana-e-pac-favelas.htm

Mbembe, A. (2006). Nècropolitique. *Raisons politiques, 21*(1), 29–60. https://doi.org/10.3917/rai.021.0029

Medeiros, F. (2018). O morto no lugar dos mortos: classificações, sistemas de controle e necropolítica no Rio de Janeiro [The dead in the place of the dead: Classifications, control systems and necropolitics in Rio de Janeiro]. *Revista M. Estudos sobre morte, os mortos e o morrer, 3*(5), 72–91. https://doi.org/10.9789/2525-3050.2018.v3i5.72-91

Mowle, T. S. (Ed.). (2007). *Hope is not a plan: The war in Iraq from inside the Green Zone.* Praeger Security International.

Nozaki, W. (2021). A Militarização da Administração Pública no Brasil: projeto de nação ou projeto de poder? [The militarisation of public administration in Brazil: Nation project or power project?]. *Caderno da Reforma Administrativa, 20.*
Pauschinger, D. (2020a). Working at the edge: Police, emotions and space in Rio de Janeiro. *Environment and Planning D: Society and Space, 38*(3), 510–527. https://doi.org/10.1177/0263775819882711
Pauschinger, D. (2020b). The permeable Olympic fortress: Mega-event security as camouflage in Rio de Janeiro. *Conflict and Society: Advances in Research, 6*(1), 108–127. https://doi.org/10.3167/arcs.2020.060107
Pauschinger, D. (2023). The triangle of security governance: Sovereignty, discipline and the 'government of things' in Olympic Rio de Janeiro. *Security Dialogue, 54*(1), 94–111. https://doi.org/10.1177/09670106221142142
Pauschinger, D. (2024). *Policing sport mega-events: Security, spectacle, and camouflage in Rio de Janeiro.* Oxford University Press.
Phillips, T. (2020a). Jair Bolsonaro's racist comment sparks outrage from indigenous groups. *The Guardian.* Retrieved March 23, 2024, from https://www.theguardian.com/world/2020/jan/24/jair-bolsonaro-racist-comment-sparks-outrage-indigenous-groups
Phillips, T. (2020b). Brazil: Bolsonaro reportedly uses homophobic slur to mock masks. *The Guardian.* Retrieved March 23, 2024, from https://www.theguardian.com/world/2020/jul/08/bolsonaro-masks-slur-brazil-coronavirus
Pougy, V., & Greenwald, G. (2019). Video: As Brazil's Jair Bolsonaro prepares to meet Donald Trump, his family's close ties to notorious paramilitary gangs draw scrutiny and outrage. *The Intercept.* Retrieved March 23, 2024, from https://theintercept.com/2019/03/18/jair-bolsonaro-family-militias-gangs-brazil/. Accessed 23 March 2024.
Richmond, M. A. (2019). "Hostages to both sides": Favela pacification as dual security assemblage. *Geoforum, 104,* 71–80. https://doi.org/10.1016/j.geoforum.2019.06.011
Rocha, C. (2019). "Imposto è Roubo!" A Formação de um Contrapúblico Ultraliberal e os Protestos Pró- Impeachment de Dilma Rousseff ["Tax is Theft!" The Formation of an Ultraliberal Counterpublic and Dilma Rousseff's Pro-Impeachment Protests]. *Dados, 62*(3), e20190076. https://doi.org/10.1590/001152582019189
SECOM (Secretariat for Social Communication of the Presidency of the Republic). (2016). Security in the Rio 2016 Olympic and Paralympic Games. Updated 18 July. http://www.brasil2016.gov.br/en/presskit/files/fact-sheet-security
Sullivan, Z. (2018). LGBTQ Brazilians on edge after self-described 'homophobic' lawmaker elected president. *NBC News.* Retrieved March 23, 2024, from https://www.nbcnews.com/feature/nbc-out/lgbtq-brazilians-edge-after-self-described-homophobic-lawmaker-elected-president-n925726
Talbot, A. (2024). *Resisting Olympic evictions: Contesting space in Rio de Janeiro.* Manchester University Press.

Walker, G. H., Stanton, N. A., Salmon, P. M., & Jenkins, D. P. (2017). *Command and control: The sociotechnical perspective*. CRC Press.

Ward, S. V. (2007). Promoting the Olympic city. In J. R. Gold & M. M. Gold (Eds.), *Olympic cities: City agendas, planning, and the world's games, 1896–2012* (pp. 120–137). Routledge.

Wolfe, S. D. (2020). 'For the benefit of our nation': Unstable soft power in the 2018 men's World Cup in Russia. *International Journal of Sport Policy and Politics*, 12(4), 545–561. https://doi.org/10.1080/19406940.2020.1839532

Zweig, S. (1942). *Brazil: Land of the future*. Cassell.

Open Access This chapter is licensed under the terms of the Creative Commons Attribution 4.0 International License (http://creativecommons.org/licenses/by/4.0/), which permits use, sharing, adaptation, distribution and reproduction in any medium or format, as long as you give appropriate credit to the original author(s) and the source, provide a link to the Creative Commons license and indicate if changes were made.

The images or other third party material in this chapter are included in the chapter's Creative Commons license, unless indicated otherwise in a credit line to the material. If material is not included in the chapter's Creative Commons license and your intended use is not permitted by statutory regulation or exceeds the permitted use, you will need to obtain permission directly from the copyright holder.

CHAPTER 8

The Eastern European Mega-Event Decade: Sports, Geopolitics, and War at the Start of the Twenty-First Century

Vitaly Kazakov and Dmitrijs Andrejevs

Abstract This chapter explores the diversity, political significance, and legacies of Eastern European countries' experiences with sports mega-events in the twenty-first century. It also discusses Russia's "mega-event decade" and draws connections between hosting and Russia's recent hostile geopolitical actions, examining its legacies in the stark geopolitical reality of the Russo-Ukrainian war. While Russia's mega-events may have impressed domestic and international publics through spectacle and prestige, it also used these events to reduce resistance to the gradual introduction of authoritarian practices domestically and hostile geopolitical actions internationally. This case warns about the uneasy connection between mega-events and authoritarian practices more broadly. Still, the increasing volume of experiences with the whole spectrum of mega-events across

V. Kazakov (✉)
Aarhus University, Aarhus, Denmark
e-mail: vitaly.kazakov@cc.au.dk

D. Andrejevs
University of Manchester, Manchester, UK

© The Author(s) 2025
S. D. Wolfe (ed.), *The Hard Edge of Soft Power*, Mega Event Planning, https://doi.org/10.1007/978-981-96-3515-3_8

Eastern Europe makes this region fascinating, as these nations continue to negotiate their international images and national identities in volatile geopolitical and economic environments.

Keywords Soft power • Authoritarianism • Hard power • Central and Eastern Europe • Russia • Mega-events

Introduction

The impressive heterogeneity of different sports mega-events that came to Eastern Europe in the twenty-first century is too broad for a single chapter. Indeed, entire volumes have studied the complexity of the region's relationship with mega-events (Makarychev & Yatsyk, 2016b). This chapter specifically discusses what could be termed the "golden age" of Eastern European mega-events, when multiple events came to the regions east of Germany. Following the collapse of the Soviet Union, many "new" countries across this region, including Russia, actively forged international images and national identities, dealing with past trauma and negotiating their place in the region and the world. Mega-events became a useful element of the larger toolbox for nation-building, international relations, and economic and political influence.

The first part of this chapter focuses on cases across Eastern Europe, while the second examines the Russian experience. The latter hosted the world's most prestigious sporting events in the 2010s, a period that has been dubbed "a Russian mega-event decade" (Wolfe, 2021). In fact, countries across the region experienced a "mega-event decade" of their own. Speaking to the themes of this book, we examine the push-and-pull dynamics associated with major sporting events. Mega-events embody the re-orientation of most countries in the region toward Western democratic and free market values. They provide a platform for international cooperation and civil activism, enable meaningful change such as improved labor laws and better inclusion for people with disabilities, and also signal the arrival onto the global arena of countries formerly in the shadow of the USSR. At the same time, just as elsewhere in the world, hosting can correlate with the (re)introduction of authoritarian practices, such as crackdowns on civil society, blatant corruption, and "sportswashing" (Boykoff, 2022; Skey, 2022; Jennings, 2013).

Sports Mega-Events and Eastern Europe

The first decade after the collapse of socialism was a time of turbulent change for the region. This included the reshaping of sports governance institutions as well as economic instability that affected the development of sport and the (in)ability of nations to host first-tier mega-events such as the FIFA World Cup or the Olympic Games (Borrero, 2017; Rojo-Labaien et al., 2020; Horne, 2017). Two decades later, the picture looked more optimistic. From the European Basketball Championship (EuroBasket), to the Universiade/World University Games, the European Games, and the World Games, cities across Eastern Europe hosted an array of prominent mega-events. While Russia was the most prolific host in the 2010s—including the 2014 Winter Olympic Games and the 2018 FIFA Men's World Cup—many other nations welcomed noteworthy sport events, including Slovakia, Poland, Hungary, Belarus, Latvia, Azerbaijan, and Kazakhstan (Müller & Pickles, 2015).

Most prominently, the UEFA Men's European Football Championship (Euro 2012) was hosted by Poland and Ukraine. In many ways, Euro 2012 opened the region to international sports spectators, as evidenced by the growth of both in-person and media audiences (Kassimeris & Kennedy, 2014). This meant that domestic and external audiences engaged with and challenged the national image projections centered around post-socialist transformations and consolidation of European statehood. After all, the Euros have been a prominent site in which contemporary European national identities were forged in the twentieth and twenty-first centuries (Mittag & Legrand, 2010; Pyta & Havemann, 2015; Ludvigsen & Petersen-Wagner, 2022).

The results from Euro 2012 were mixed due to the preexisting conceptions of host nations, domestic and urban politics, and the interplay between modalities of soft power (e.g., Makarychev & Yatsyk, 2016a; Kowalska, 2017; Rek-Woźniak & Woźniak, 2020). While direct experiences with the championship led to some positive image returns for Poland, locals experienced the emotional patterns associated with mega-events highlighted in the introduction to this volume (e.g., Dembek & Włoch, 2014; Jaskulowski & Surmiak, 2016). Specifically, despite the political elites' endorsement, the "feel-good factor" did not extend to the Polish-Slovakian bid for the Winter 2022 Olympic Games and it was ultimately derailed through a referendum in Kraków, signaling public apprehension due to financial and environmental concerns (Woźniak, 2019;

Mazurkiewicz, 2021). As elsewhere in the world, Eastern Europe has not been immune to the tensions between authorities' search for soft power, escalating costs, and local protest, though this did not prevent Kraków-Małopolska from hosting the European Games in 2023.

Tensions were even more pronounced for Belarus at the time of the IIHF 2014 Ice Hockey World Championship. If controversies around the imprisonment of former Ukrainian Prime Minister Yulia Tymoshenko complicated the desired effects of Euro 2012, the persistent label of the "last dictatorship in Europe" was an even bigger challenge for Belarusian image management and the Lukashenko-led government (Nizhnikau & Alvari, 2016; Rodríguez-Díaz, 2020). On the surface, this tournament was an organizational success. However, behind the Potemkin façade of "modern Belarus" lay the scaffolding of authoritarian practices, such as preventative arrests, evictions, and excessive policing (Nizhnikau & Alvari, 2016). A product of a particular blend of domestic and international agendas, the projections of "Belarusian-ness" were sensitive to the geopolitics of the moment. With Russia's actions in Crimea and eastern Ukraine, the Lukashenko regime made concessions toward a "soft Belarusization"—aimed at articulating a clearer demarcation between Belarusians and Russians—and scaled down authoritarian tactics for the European Games in 2019 (Bekus, 2023).

Belarus was stripped of co-hosting rights for the 2021 IIHF Championship after the authorities' crackdown on protests in 2020, reversing the image of European alignment. Instead, Latvia became the sole host. This tournament further highlighted increasing geopolitical tensions in the region as well as the limits of directing mega-event soft power capital for (geo)political purposes. In the host city, these tensions were reflected by the Mayor of Riga and the Latvian Minister of Foreign Affairs, replacing the flag of Belarus with the historic white-red-white flag of the Belarusian opposition. Similarly, the Russian flag was replaced with the flag of the Russian Olympic Committee during the fallout of their doping scandal. Following Russia's invasion of Ukraine in February 2022, the absence of the Russian flag continued: Russia lost hosting rights for the 2023 IIHF Championship and its national team was suspended. Indeed, there is an uneasy relationship between "soft power aspirations in the context of hard power constraints" (Wolfe, 2020, p. 545) during the last decade of mega-events in this part of the world. After all, while Russia launched its soft power project with the Winter Olympics in Sochi, it was its hard power ambitions that curtailed the hosting of the EuroBasket 2015 or the co-hosting of EuroBasket 2025 in Ukraine.

Over the last two decades, there has been an increasing desire to bid for and host the whole spectrum of mega-events across Eastern Europe. As highlighted by rumors of another joint Swedish-Latvian bid for the 2030 Winter Games or a recurring Polish and Hungarian interest in the Olympics (Bergs, 2023), the experience with second- and third-tier competitions and the prestige of hosting international sporting events continues to fuel ever-greater aspirations. These aspirations and indeed abilities to host diverge across the region and over time. Not dissimilar to their Western counterparts, the correlation between financial resources and political capital both domestically and internationally continues to shape the region's geopolitical economy of sport (see Chadwick et al., 2023).

Perhaps this relationship is strongest even further east across the former republics of the Soviet Union with, for instance, the Asian Winter Games in Kazakhstan, Formula One Baku Grand Prix in Azerbaijan, or the Asian Indoor and Martial Art Games in Turkmenistan (e.g., Nurmakov, 2016; Horák, 2016; Gogishvili, 2023). However, a more detailed discussion of these cases would require more space for reflection and a broader account of the role of "post-Soviet presidentialism" (see Rek-Woźniak & Woźniak, 2020). As in the case of Belarus or Russia, a closer examination is required of the role of autocratic leadership, modes of nation-state-building, and the role of Potemkinism when it comes to mega-events within the specificities of this region. The uneasy correlation between degrees of (il)liberality of the regime and the scale and density of the sport calendar is not exclusive to the easternmost European countries either (UoM, 2022). For example, Hungary might be among the most active host countries in the region over the last decade, while the regime led by Viktor Orbán is at the forefront of the "illiberal turn" within the European Union (Garamvölgyi & Dóczi, 2021).

Just as with Belarus, the push-and-pull effects of the European Union and Russia must be considered. In the end, the desire for European and international recognition—however contradictory the process may be—is one of the key facets of the Eastern European mega-event experience. Ultimately, the region illuminates the relationship between applying for and hosting mega-events alongside the complexities of the political fluctuations between internal autocratic and democratic trends, and external geopolitical entanglements.

THE RUSSIAN CASE

Few other cases illustrate these complexities as well as Russia in the twenty-first century, which became one of the world's main mega-event powers by hosting two first-tier sporting events. In the mid-2000s, the Russian state found a new level of stability and prosperity, coming at the price of building the so-called power vertical with President Putin at the helm, and gradual encroachment on media and personal freedoms (Gelman & Ryzhenkov, 2012). Whether by chance or by design, mega-events turned out to be a significant part of the Kremlin's strategy to engage domestic and foreign audiences in the 2000s and 2010s. They presented a convenient option not only to claim great world power status—a Kremlin aspiration since the collapse of the USSR—but to enact it performatively through the prestige of hosting (Petersson, 2014).

The utilization of major sports projects served a dual purpose for the government. For instance, the 2018 Men's FIFA World Cup allowed authorities to claim they were upgrading "essential infrastructures in the host cities while crafting a presentation of the nation as competent and modern … a transformative, utopian vision" (Wolfe, 2021, 145). This is the essence of a new Potemkinism, "wherein officials worked to create and distribute a superficial construction (of neoliberal change, for example, or international integration) while maintaining the status quo underneath that surface" (Wolfe, 2021, p. 153). Regarding the Kremlin's engagement with mega-events, this discussion traces the overlaps between internal political context and external geopolitical developments.

That mega-events were part of the Russian government's wider strategy is evident from the fact that Russia submitted a bid to host the 2012 Summer Olympic Games in Moscow during Putin's first presidential term in 2003. The bid was unsuccessful, losing to London and coming behind other major Western capital cities. When assessing Moscow's bid, however, the International Olympic Committee (IOC)s evaluation report noted that the proposed Olympics "would occur in a country which is establishing itself as the 'New Russia'," and that the bid was backed by "77% support in Moscow and 76% support throughout Russia" (IOC, 2005, 46–47). Despite being unsuccessful, this bid hinted at the dual aim of hosting that would underpin Russia's overall mega-event strategy: attempting to impress foreign audiences with a vision of a new Russia, while galvanizing domestic support for the regime (Kazakov, 2019). Notably, the IOC evaluation report highlighted that popular support for the London and New York Olympic bids was significantly lower than for Moscow (IOC, 2005).

Russia's efforts proved successful in the 2014 Olympic bidding process. Again promising to deliver a "new Russia" to Olympic audiences, members of the IOC were swayed to vote for Sochi partly thanks to Putin's personal backing of the bid and his rare English-language speech at the IOC congress. Upon learning of the success of Sochi's bid, Putin stated: "[t]his is, without a doubt not only a recognition of Russia's achievements in sports, it is [...] an assessment of our country. [...] This is an acknowledgment of its growing capabilities, first and foremost in the *economic and social spheres*" (quoted in Kishkovsky, 2007, emphasis added). While not exclusive to Russia, the interplay between the search for international recognition through mega-events under the backing of a charismatic leader became a feature of post-Soviet presidentialism (Rojo-Labaien et al., 2020). Soon after, FIFA chose Russia to host the 2018 Football World Cup. These IOC and FIFA endorsements symbolically reconfirmed the country's entrance into an elite club of international powers hosting first-tier mega-events.

Because of the timescales required to prepare for hosting, the country that ends up staging the event may—in a sense—not be the same country that bid for it initially. In the case of Russia, much had changed between the mid-2000s and mid-2010s. Notably, Putin returned to the presidency after a term as prime minister. Much of the preparatory stages, including the rhetorical construction of the "new Russia" in the bid books and progress reports ahead of the 2014 Olympics and 2018 World Cup, took place within the "modernization" discourse and Western orientation of Medvedev's presidency (Kazakov, 2019; Wolfe, 2021). The Russia that hosted the two mega-events—as opposed to the Russia that bid—pivoted toward narratives of the so-called traditional family values (Sharafutdinova, 2014), and thus contrasted sharply with the bids' rhetoric of Western-style modernization. The organization process ahead of the Sochi Olympics was also far from smooth. Accusations of homophobia and decreasing space for protest amid a crackdown on media and civil freedoms, joined by concerns around corruption, challenged the official messaging by the government and the IOC (Gronskaya & Makarychev, 2014).

The discourse around the Sochi Games' legacy was shaped not by the spectacle of the mega-event itself, but by two major related stories: the doping scandal and the annexation of Crimea. The latter promoted Russian power narratives adopted by the Kremlin, in a way that was similar to the Sochi Olympics: both official discourses adopted securitization logic and embodied the desire to demonstrate strength, reclaim great power status, consolidate Russian society, and promote sovereignty (Makarychev & Yatsyk, 2014). That Russian athletes and sport administrators resorted to state-sponsored doping to achieve impressive results in Sochi was also interpreted through a biopolitics lens, as government efforts to influence the Games via illegal control over athletes' bodies and performances (Makarychev & Medvedev, 2019). The Crimea and doping affairs both demonstrate a striking similarity in method that was condemned internationally. The decision not to award the 2019 European Games to Russia in the wake of the doping scandal (AP, 2016) was one of the manifestations of the tarnished status of the recent Olympic host.

Yet, the Sochi Games served as a useful training ground for Russian organizers, who used this experience to stage the FIFA tournament across multiple major cities in western Russia and reach a global audience through the world's most popular game. Like Sochi, the World Cup served as an extension of local, regional, national, and international Russian politics and societal issues (see Arnold, 2021a; Wolfe, 2021). Among them were concerns around the use of modernization rhetoric to justify the megaevent as a "security laboratory." The introduction of new regulatory mechanisms around alcohol consumption, urban mobility, leisure activities, and food quality was justified necessary for organizing an international spectacle. The Russian authorities tested out "technologies of creating politically sterile and simultaneously secure spaces of total control and supervision that might be replicated elsewhere—in hosting cultural festivities and political summits, or neutralizing street demonstrations" (Ipek & Makarychev, 2021, p. 47). Wolfe argued that these practices were the culmination of the Potemkin nature of the World Cup and the opportunities it provided to advance domestic soft power (Wolfe, 2021; Arnold, 2021b). Further attempts to boost popular support for the ruling regime were made through staging a variety of smaller-scale sports and entertainment events, from the 2013 Kazan Universiade, to the 2017 World Festival of Youth and Students in Sochi, to the Yekaterinburg University International Sports Festival in 2023—the inaugural alternative to the FISU World University Games (Makarychev & Yatsyk, 2016b; Koivunen, 2021).

In the international realm, unlike in the aftermath of Sochi, "Russia's hosting of the World Cup became both a defining and a defying act for Putin—it defined the country's geopolitical status and was a defiant geopolitical triumph" (Foxall, 2021, 181). It was arguably the pinnacle of the Potemkinist approach to Russian politics in the twenty-first century. It may be a coincidence that Russia's major geopolitical conflicts were timed in close proximity to major mega-events. Still, shortly after Russia was awarded the 2014 Games, and just before the opening of the Beijing 2008 Olympics, the Russo-Georgian War broke out. Further, the Crimean annexation immediately followed the closing of the 2014 Games. Later, Russia's involvement in the Syrian civil war, as well as the ongoing war in Donbas, provided the backdrop for the 2018 World Cup. And finally, according to some media reports, the start of the Russian invasion of Ukraine in 2022 was delayed due to China's Winter Olympics (Wong & Barnes, 2022). All these may indeed be coincidental. Yet that Russian officials expressed interest in submitting a bid for the Euro 2028 Football tournament in the wake of the invasion of Ukraine signaled that the Kremlin continued to view mega-events as a tool to engage with global and domestic audiences. Whether this promptly rejected bid was a product of delusion or cynicism on the part of Russian sports authorities remains unclear (Braidwood, 2022). Even after the Ukraine invasion, mega-events have served as a tool for the Kremlin to achieve two goals: to showcase a "new Russia" and impress domestic and international publics through spectacle and prestige, and to reduce resistance to the gradual introduction of authoritarian practices domestically and hostile geopolitical actions internationally.

CONCLUSIONS

The story of major sporting events in Eastern Europe in the twenty-first century mirrors the profound political and social changes of this region in the turbulent post-Soviet era. However, mega-events in the Russian national context are not representative of the region as a whole. We do not suggest, based on lessons learned from Russia in the 2010s, that hosting inevitably leads to an authoritarian slide or geopolitical war. Instead, this case warns us about the uneasy link between mega-events and authoritarian practices more broadly: not just in domestic politics, but also in international governance including the sporting sphere. Some Western journalists who praised the 2018 World Cup after the event have since questioned the role of international sporting bodies in choosing mega-event hosts and their complicity in how Russian politics have unfolded during the mega-event decade (Ronay, 2022).

Ultimately, the suspension of hosting rights for the 2022 UEFA Men's Champions League final in Saint Petersburg and the Sochi Formula One Grand Prix, as well as shrinking of the previously pan-regional Kontinental Hockey League, demonstrates how the legacy of Russia's mega-event decade has crumbled in the wake of the Kremlin's geopolitical decisions and internal policies. Russia's rejected bid for Euro 2028 and subsequent discussions about leaving UEFA in favor of the Asian Football Confederation underline the enduring search for international status and domestic legitimacy through mega-events, even in times of war (Mikhailov, 2022; Kazakov, 2024). Given the bans on participation in major European competitions, de-facto alternatives to the Summer 2024 Olympics (such as the 2024 World Friendship Games or the 2024 BRICS Games) likewise underscore the Russian government's continuous reliance on mega-events in international relations and domestic policies in the post-Ukraine invasion era.

At the same time, other countries east of Germany continue to host major European competitions with greater frequency, which puts them on the same footing as their Western counterparts. Nevertheless, there continues to be a qualitative divide between the two within the sporting universe. An argument for a "second-tier Europeanness" could be made through the lens of the UEFA competitions here. For example, while five Europa League finals took place in Eastern Europe since 2011, only one UEFA Champions League final took place in the region within the same timeframe.

The increasing frequency of the co-hosting model and recent participation of Azerbaijan, Romania, Hungary, and Russia in UEFA Euro 2020's staging keeps open the question of major international sports bodies' role in "Europeanization" or Westernization through mega-events. What unites the countries across the region, however, is that while the Western states experience diminishing enthusiasm about the envisioned returns on investment in the soft power, social, and economic effects of mega-events (e.g., Chappelet, 2021), their Eastern neighbors remain more optimistic about the mobilization of sports capital for the benefit of promoting more favorable international images and achieving internal political goals.

While Russia is the only country within the region to host the Olympic Games or the Football World Cup, the growing experiences with second- and third-tier events are perhaps indicative of more prestigious mega-events to come (Rojo-Labaien, 2023; Gogishvili & Harris-Brandts, 2022). The abrupt withdrawal of Russia and Belarus from the pool of mega-event hosts could open doors for some of the rising players in the region, such as Hungary and Poland, or Azerbaijan, Kazakhstan, and Turkey further east, as well as Ukraine in its eventual post-war recovery. However, the complexities of the latest Nagorno-Karabakh conflict in the Caucasus, recent civil unrest in Kazakhstan, and the ongoing impact of the war on Ukraine and its European neighbors will all continue to shape the region's engagement with mega-events.

References

AP. (2016, January 21). Russia Still "preferred Host" for 2019 European Games. *USA Today.* https://www.usatoday.com/story/sports/olympics/2016/01/21/russia-still-preferred-host-for-2019-european-games/79110496/
Arnold, R. (Ed.). (2021a). *Russia and the 2018 FIFA World Cup.* Routledge.
Arnold, R. (2021b). Sport and domestic "soft power" in Russia: Take the skinheads bowling. In R. Arnold (Ed.), *Russia and the 2018 FIFA World Cup* (pp. 100–117). Routledge.
Bekus, N. (2023). Reassembling society in a nation-state: History, language, and identity discourses of Belarus. *Nationalities Papers, 51*(1), 98–113. https://doi.org/10.1017/nps.2022.60
Bergs, M. (2023, March 10). Latvia and Sweden considering joint Winter Olympic Bid. *LSM.lv.* https://eng.lsm.lv/article/culture/sport/10.03.2023-latvia-and-sweden-considering-joint-winter-olympic-bid.a500169/
Borrero, M. (2017). Sport in Russia and Eastern Europe. In R. Edelman & W. Wilson (Eds.), *The Oxford handbook of sport history* (pp. 319–330). Oxford University Press. https://academic.oup.com/edited-volume/28367/chapter/215245702
Boykoff, J. (2022). Toward a theory of sportswashing: Mega-events, soft power, and political conflict. *Sociology of Sport Journal, 39*(4), 342–351. https://doi.org/10.1123/ssj.2022-0095
Braidwood, J. (2022, May 2). Russia banned from making Euro 2028 bid as part of Uefa measures. *The Independent.* https://www.independent.co.uk/sport/football/russia-uefa-euros-2028-bid-b2069982.html
Chadwick, S., Widdop, P., & Goldman, M. M. (Eds.). (2023). *The geopolitical economy of sport: Power, politics, money, and the state.* Routledge.
Chappelet, J.-L. (2021). Winter Olympic referendums: Reasons for opposition to the games. *The International Journal of the History of Sport, 38*(13–14), 1369–1384. https://doi.org/10.1080/09523367.2021.1997997
Dembek, A., & Włoch, R. (2014). The impact of a sports mega-event on the international image of a country: The case of Poland hosting UEFA Euro 2012. *Perspectives, 22*(1), 33–47.

Foxall, A. (2021). Vladimir Putin, Russian foreign policy, and the 2018 FIFA World Cup: Making Russia great again. In R. Arnold (Ed.), *Russia and the 2018 FIFA World Cup* (pp. 169–186). Routledge.

Garamvölgyi, B., & Dóczi, T. (2021). Sport as a tool for public diplomacy in Hungary. *Physical Culture and Sport. Studies and Research, 90*(1), 39–49.

Gelman, V., & Ryzhenkov, S. (2012). Local regimes, sub-national governance and the 'power vertical' in contemporary Russia. In C. Ross (Ed.), *Russian regional politics under Putin and Medvedev*. Routledge.

Gogishvili, D. (2023). Mega-event on the streets: The Formula 1 Grand Prix in Baku, Azerbaijan. In D. Sturm, S. Wagg, & D. L. Andrews (Eds.), *The history and politics of motor racing: Lives in the fast lane* (pp. 665–690). Palgrave Macmillan. https://doi.org/10.1007/978-3-031-22825-4_26

Gogishvili, D., & Harris-Brandts, S. (2022). Urban impacts of second-tier mega-events in the Global East: The European youth Olympic festival in Tbilisi and Baku. In N. C. Hanakata, F. Bignami, & N. Cuppini (Eds.), *Mega events, urban transformations and social citizenship* (pp. 136–152). Routledge.

Gronskaya, N., & Makarychev, A. (2014). The 2014 Sochi Olympics and "sovereign power". *Problems of post-communism, 61*(1), 41–51. https://doi.org/10.2753/PPC1075-8216610103

Horák, S. (2016). Nation-building and sporting spectacles in authoritarian regimes: Turkmenistan's Aziada- 2017. In N. Koch (Ed.), *Critical geographies of sport: Space, power and sport in global perspective* (pp. 48–63). Routledge.

Horne, J. (2017). Sports mega-events—Three sites of contemporary political contestation. *Sport in Society, 20*(3), 328–340. https://doi.org/10.1080/17430437.2015.1088721

IOC. (2005). *Report of the IOC evaluation commission for the games of the XXX Olympiad in 2012*. Lausanne, Switzerland: International Olympic Committee. https://stillmed.olympics.com/media/Document%20Library/OlympicOrg/Documents/Host-City-Elections/XXX-Olympiad-2012/Report-of-the-IOC-Evaluation-Commission-for-the-Games-of-the-XXX-Olympiad-2012.pdf

Ipek, V., & Makarychev, A. (2021). Security and the spectacle: The 2018 FIFA World Cup in Russia's "safest City". In R. Arnold (Ed.), *Russia and the 2018 FIFA World Cup* (pp. 33–55). Routledge.

Jaskulowski, K., & Surmiak, A. (2016). Social construction of the impact of Euro 2012: A Wroclaw case study. *Leisure Studies, 35*(5), 600–615. https://doi.org/10.1080/02614367.2015.1037790

Jennings, W. (2013). Governing the games: High politics, risk and mega-events. *Political Studies Review, 11*(1), 2–14. https://doi.org/10.1111/1478-9302.12002

Kassimeris, C., & Kennedy, P. (2014). Introduction to special issue: Exploring the cultural, ideological and economic legacies of Euro 2012. *Soccer & Society, 15*(2), 177–189. https://doi.org/10.1080/14660970.2013.849185

Kazakov, V. (2019). Representations of "New Russia" through a 21st century mega-event: The political aims, informational means, and popular reception of the Sochi 2014 Winter Olympic Games (PhD Dissertation). Manchester, UK: The University of Manchester.

Kazakov, V. (2024). Russian elite sports policy in the 21st century. In J. Grix, P. M. Brannagan, & B. Houlihan (Eds.), *Comparative elite sport development* (2nd ed.). Routledge.

Kishkovsky, S. (2007). After celebrating winning bid, Russia has work ahead. http://www.nytimes.com/2007/07/06/sports/06olympics.html

Koivunen, P. (2021). International events in the service of cultural statecraft: The Sochi Olympics and the world festival of youth and students. In T. Forsberg & S. Mäkinen (Eds.), *Russia's cultural statecraft* (pp. 184–205). Routledge.

Kowalska, M. Z. (2017). *Urban politics of a sporting mega event: Legitimacy and legacy of Euro 2012 in anthropological perspective.* Palgrave Macmillan.

Ludvigsen, J. A. L., & Petersen-Wagner, R. (2022). *The UEFA European football championships: Politics, media spectacle and social change.* Routledge. https://doi.org/10.4324/9781003359098

Makarychev, A., & Medvedev, S. (2019). Doped and disclosed: Anatomopolitics, biopower, and sovereignty in the Russian sports industry. *Politics and the Life Sciences, 38*(2), 132–143. https://www.cambridge.org/core/journals/politics-and-the-life-sciences/article/abs/doped-and-disclosed/F6AA8C2548A9DAFE1CE67DC38DF0CC96

Makarychev, A., & Yatsyk, A. (2014). The four pillars of Russia's power narrative. *The International Spectator, 49*(4), 62–75.

Makarychev, A., & Yatsyk, A. (2016a). Both in-between and out: National sovereignty and cross-border governmentality in Euro 2012 in Lviv. In B. Bruns, D. Happ, & H. Zichner (Eds.), *European neighbourhood policy: Geopolitics between integration and security* (pp. 93–114). Palgrave Macmillan. https://doi.org/10.1057/978-1-349-69504-1_5

Makarychev, A., & Yatsyk, A. (2016b). *Mega events in post-Soviet Eurasia: Shifting borderlines of inclusion and exclusion.* Palgrave Macmillan.

Mazurkiewicz, M. (2021). The games that never happened: Social reception and press coverage of the Kraków bid for the 2022 Winter Olympics (2012–2014). *The International Journal of the History of Sport, 38*(13–14), 1350–1368. https://doi.org/10.1080/09523367.2021.1997998

Mikhailov, A. (2022, December 5). 'Kak RFS Mozhet Stat' Chlenom Aziatskoī Konfederatsii Futbola'. *TACC.* https://tass.ru/sport/16482285

Mittag, J., & Legrand, B. (2010). Towards a Europeanization of football? Historical phases in the evolution of the UEFA European Football Championship. *Soccer & Society, 11*(6), 709–722. https://doi.org/10.1080/14660970.2010.510727

Müller, M., & Pickles, J. (2015). Global games, local rules: Mega-events in the post-Socialist world. *European Urban and Regional Studies, 22*(2), 121–127. https://doi.org/10.1177/0969776414560866

Nizhnikau, R., & Alvari, N. (2016). Ice Hockey World Championship in Belarus: Political context. In A. Makarychev & A. Yatsyk (Eds.), *Mega events in post-Soviet Eurasia: Shifting borderlines of inclusion and exclusion* (pp. 79–97). Palgrave Macmillan. https://doi.org/10.1057/978-1-137-49095-7_5

Nurmakov, A. (2016). Kazakhstan and the global industry of mega events: A case of autocratic management. In A. Makarychev & A. Yatsyk (Eds.), *Mega events in post-Soviet Eurasia: Shifting Borderlines of Inclusion and Exclusion* (pp. 99–129). Palgrave Macmillan. https://doi.org/10.1057/978-1-137-49095-7_6

Petersson, B. (2014). Still embodying the myth? Russia's recognition as a great power and the Sochi Winter Games. *Problems of Post-Communism, 61*(1), 30–42.

Pyta, W., & Havemann, N. (Eds.). (2015). *European Football and collective memory*. Palgrave Macmillan.

Rek-Woźniak, M., & Woźniak, W. (2020). BBC's documentary "stadiums of hate" and manufacturing of the News: Case study in moral panics and media manipulation. *Journal of Sport and Social Issues, 44*(6), 515–533. https://doi.org/10.1177/0193723519899244

Rodríguez-Díaz, Á. (2020). Sport in the political and economic transition in Belarus: State nationalism and mega events. In E. Rojo-Labaien, Á. Rodríguez-Díaz, & J. Rookwood (Eds.), *Sport, Statehood and Transition in Europe* (pp. 179–197). Routledge.

Rojo-Labaien, E. (2023). Azerbaijan on the crossroad between Eastern and Western State building: The Baku 2015 European games and the boundaries of Europe. *Sport in Society, 26*(4), 650–670. https://doi.org/10.1080/17430437.2022.2033217

Rojo-Labaien, E., Díaz, Á. R., & Rookwood, J. (Eds.). (2020). *Sport, statehood and transition in Europe: Comparative perspectives from post-Soviet and post-socialist societies*. Routledge.

Ronay, B. (2022, February 25). 'Uefa and Fifa are too late: Russia's sportswashing has served its purpose. *The Guardian*, sec. Football. https://www.theguardian.com/football/2022/feb/25/uefa-and-fifa-are-too-late-russias-sportswashing-has-served-its-purpose

Sharafutdinova, G. (2014). The pussy riot affair and Putin's dèmarche from sovereign democracy to sovereign morality. *Nationalities Papers, 42*(4), 615–621.

Skey, M. (2022). Sportswashing: Media headline or analytic concept? *International Review for the Sociology of Sport, 58*(5), 1–16. https://doi.org/10.1177/10126902221136086

UoM. (2022). (Il)Liberal nation projection through sport, culture, entertainment, and international broadcasting. https://research.manchester.ac.uk/en/activities/illiberal-nation-projection-through-sport-culture-entertainment-a

Wolfe, S. D. (2020). "For the benefit of our nation": Unstable soft power in the 2018 Men's World Cup in Russia. *International Journal of Sport Policy and Politics, 12*(4), 545–561. https://doi.org/10.1080/19406940.2020.1839532

Wolfe, S. D. (2021). *More than sport: Soft power and Potemkinism in the 2018 Men's Football World Cup in Russia*. LIT Verlag Münster.

Wong, E., & Julian, B. (2022, March 2). China asked Russia to delay Ukraine war until after Olympics, U.S. officials say. *The New York Times*. https://www.nytimes.com/2022/03/02/us/politics/russia-ukraine-china.html

Woźniak, W. (2019). Politics, sport mega events and grassroots mobilization. Anticipated triumph and unexpected failure of political elite in Poland. *Communist and Post-Communist Studies, 52*(4), 367–378. https://doi.org/10.1016/j.postcomstud.2019.10.002

Open Access This chapter is licensed under the terms of the Creative Commons Attribution 4.0 International License (http://creativecommons.org/licenses/by/4.0/), which permits use, sharing, adaptation, distribution and reproduction in any medium or format, as long as you give appropriate credit to the original author(s) and the source, provide a link to the Creative Commons license and indicate if changes were made.

The images or other third party material in this chapter are included in the chapter's Creative Commons license, unless indicated otherwise in a credit line to the material. If material is not included in the chapter's Creative Commons license and your intended use is not permitted by statutory regulation or exceeds the permitted use, you will need to obtain permission directly from the copyright holder.

CHAPTER 9

The Salt Lake City 2002 Winter Olympics: Soft Power, Sportswashing, and the Invasion of Iraq

Jules Boykoff and Reed McFeely

Abstract This chapter examines the 2002 Salt Lake City Winter Olympics as a means to think through the relationship between soft power and hard power. Salt Lake City 2002 often gets attention for its jaw-dropping corruption and the introduction of new mega-event-related security regimes. But, as the first Olympics after the 9/11 terrorist attacks, the Games took on new meaning at the nexus of soft power, sportswashing, and the eventual invasion of Iraq. With Los Angeles hosting the 2028 Olympics and Salt Lake City on track to stage the 2034 Winter Games, a frank and frontal look at the past can illuminate key political dynamics in play today.

Keywords Soft power • Hard power • Geopolitics • Sportswashing • United States • Olympics

J. Boykoff (✉) • R. McFeely
Pacific University, Forest Grove, OR, USA
e-mail: boyk1563@pacificu.edu

© The Author(s) 2025
S. D. Wolfe (ed.), *The Hard Edge of Soft Power*, Mega Event Planning, https://doi.org/10.1007/978-981-96-3515-3_9

Introduction

The 2002 Salt Lake City Winter Olympics were staged only five months after the 9/11 terrorist attacks. The US security machine was humming in overdrive. The US population was on high alert. At the Games' opening ceremony, US President George W. Bush officially kicked off the Olympics by stating, "On behalf of a proud, determined, and grateful nation, I declare open the Games of Salt Lake City, celebrating the Olympic Winter Games" (The White House, 2002). Despite the seemingly prosaic nature of the statement, his words caused an international kerfuffle in Olympic circles. After all, the standard opening for a Winter Olympics, as engraved in the Olympic Charter, was "I declare open the Games of (name of City), celebrating the Olympic Winter Games" (International Olympic Committee, 2001, p. 94). Many interpreted the US president's conspicuous addition as laced with a mèlange of resilience and menace. As *Newsweek* put it at the time, "Perhaps more than ever, these games are about more than sport. And with his largest TV audience ever, Bush decided to send an international message" (Brant, 2012).

At that same opening ceremony, eight US Olympians formed an honor guard alongside New York police and firefighters as well as members of the Port Authority police. They gingerly toted a tattered US flag that had been retrieved from the wreckage of New York City's World Trade Center. Silence descended on the 50,000 in attendance. International Olympic Committee (IOC) President Jacques Rogge then said, "People of America, Utah, and Salt Lake City, we are gathered once again in your great country." The Belgian Count added, "Your nation is overcoming a horrific tragedy, a tragedy that has affected the whole world. We stand united with you in promoting our common ideas and hope for world peace" (Roberts, 2002, A1). Yoav Dubinsky (2019) asserts that Olympic opening ceremonies are particularly efficient conductors of soft power, often promulgating cultural ideals.

As the world's biggest sports, media, and marketing event, the Olympics are, *par excellence*, an instance of soft power in action. Political scientist Joseph Nye (2004, p. 5) asserts that soft power "rests on the ability to shape the preferences of others" through attraction rather than coercion. Soft power involves pulling people toward one's values and ideas rather than forcing their compliance through hard-power modes like military threats or economic sanctions. It is rooted in constructive enticement rather than blunt military muscle. Wolfe (2020, p. 547) states that sports mega-events "reveal that soft and hard powers are not necessarily so opposed as imagined: they can intermingle, sometimes complementing one another, sometimes contradicting." He adds, "Hard and soft powers are contingent and mutable, engaged by heterogeneous methods at various times and dependent on a variety of actors, targets, and contextual conditions."

Sometimes, soft power and hard power go hand in hand. President Bush's breach of Olympic protocol demonstrated how the soft power inherent to the Olympic project can be subtly tweaked into a discursive bridge toward the brass-knuckle execution of hard power. The Salt Lake City Olympics and all the socio-political scaffolding around the event not only chimed with but advanced the discursive juggernaut that culminated in the US invasion of Iraq only 405 days later. These dynamics fit snugly inside the parameters of sportswashing: when political leaders use sport as a legitimate lever on the global stage while ramping up nationalism and parrying attention away from domestic human rights issues (Boykoff, 2022; Grix et al., 2023).

THE 2002 SALT LAKE CITY OLYMPICS: SCANDAL AND SECURITY SPECTACLE

The 2002 Salt Lake City Winter Olympics might be best known for the jaw-dropping bribery scandal that preceded them. In November 1998, local journalists in Utah revealed sweeping corruption. A special US Senate investigation chaired by George J. Mitchell uncovered more than 1375 separate expenditures totaling nearly $3 million that the Salt Lake City bid team disbursed to cajole support from IOC members (Mitchell et al., 1999, p. 9). The son of Libyan IOC member Bashir Mohamed Attarabulsi got free tuition to attend Brigham Young University and a local community college, plus $700 monthly payments. Congolese IOC member Jean-Claude Ganga secured more than $250,000 worth of gifts: his mother-in-law scored a knee replacement, his wife received cosmetic surgery, and he underwent treatment for hepatitis. Salt Lake City bidders also doled out cash (Wenn et al., 2011, pp. 46–47; Sullivan, 1999).

Still, the Games went on. Salt Lake City organizers hired Mitt Romney to take the helm. The venture capitalist, who was also a devout Mormon graduate of Brigham Young University, teamed up with Salt Lake City's progressive mayor, Rocky Anderson, who later stated, "Mitt did an absolutely fantastic job" (Springer, 2015). For its part, the IOC hired the PR firm Hill and Knowlton, notorious for fabricating a Kuwaiti girl's testimony in front of a US congressional committee in the 1990s that vilified Saddam Hussain and Iraq (Knightley, 2001). The IOC also suspended six members ensnared in the scandal, eventually expelling them. Four additional IOC members chose to resign (Wenn et al., 2011). The IOC also created an Ethics Commission, which submits its findings and recommendations to an IOC Executive Board that has the final say (Chappelet, 2008), and brought on Henry Kissinger as an "Honor Member" in 2000.

The Salt Lake City Olympics were heavily securitized. During the Games, more US soldiers were on duty in Salt Lake City than Afghanistan (Baxter, 2002). Organizers requested billions in federal government funds to securitize the Games (Romney, 2004, pp. 226, 234). In the end, US taxpayers contributed $1.5 billion toward the Olympics, with around $335 million going toward security, constituting 1.5 times more than the US Treasury had spent on all seven previous US Olympics combined (Bartlett & Steele, 2001; Gerlach, 2008, p. 144). A reported 12,000 security officials guarded the Games, armed with biometric surveillance technologies, chemical weapons, riot gear, and less-lethal weapons for crowd dispersion. Olympic organizers created "designated forums" where activists could protest so long as they obtained permits. Planned even before the 9/11 attacks, these specified protest areas were eventually called "public forum zones." Less than a month before the Olympics started, Salt Lake City's local government passed an ordinance prohibiting protesters from wearing masks in public during the Games. Nevertheless, activists staged sporadic protests in parks, streets, and "public forum zones" to raise environmental concerns and to question the use of public money on a sports mega-event instead of chronic local social problems. US security officials even assigned Olympic skiers protective FBI agents, positioned sharpshooters on mountaintops, deployed F-16 fighter jets to patrol the skies, installed an advanced network of closed security cameras, and had a stockpile of anti-anthrax on hand in case of a terrorist attack (Atkinson & Young, 2002; Gerlach, 2008).

Meanwhile, President Bush revved up the soft-power machine. The *New York Times* quoted Bush speaking to the US Olympic team: "These games come at the perfect time for us. ... It is a chance for the world to see that at a time of war, we can come together in friendly competition" (Sanger, 2002). Bush concluded by saying, "Let's roll," a nod to Todd Beamer, one of the passengers who attempted to regain control of United

Airlines flight 93 on September 11, 2001. *CNN* also reported that he told athletes, "I can't wait for Americans to see our flag fly. It is such a proud moment for all of us. This nation is steadfast and unified, and you, the athletes, are going to represent us with such class and dignity and courage" ("Olympic Games to Kick Off", 2002).

The opening ceremony served as another device in Bush's soft-power toolkit. As Matt Fawlty (2002) of *The Australian* noted, "President George W Bush abandoned his war cabinet to make the opening of the XIXth Winter Olympics a statement of good over evil, to demand these Games become a celebration of US muscle on snow and ice." The opening ceremony also exhibited a textbook example of Indigenous redwashing, wherein those in power conceal the history of colonialism in favor of portraying themselves as gracious sponsors of Indigenous culture (Millington et al., 2019). The *New York Times* wrote that Utah's Indigenous nations—the Goshute, Navajo, Paiute, Shoshone, and Ute peoples—would "get their 15 minutes" of recognition by performing during the opening ceremony before relinquishing their hotel rooms to International Olympic Committee Members, having their Olympic passes invalidated, and returning home. Clifford Duncan, a Northern Ute Nation elder, noted that Indigenous participation, if brief, was both an honor and "a small token in a way" (Wise, 2002a). This "small token" paid big soft-power dividends, conveying unity and harmony.

Perhaps the most overt display of soft-power symbology was not from Bush or the Olympic opening ceremony but rather the hyper-securitization of the Games. Scholar Bradley Congelio (2021, p. 130) details the wide-reaching extent of five-ring security processes: "The local government bulldozed local homeless encampments under the justification of 'security' and a 'beautification process'." The mayor of Las Vegas accused Salt Lake City of shipping unhoused people to Nevada. Other displaced people were moved to an abandoned mattress factory, hidden from the view of tourists but allowing those displaced to see the "Olympic sites with their twinkling lights and expensive restaurants" (Leduff, 2002, D1). However, not everyone was as critical. Mike Boger, a sheriff from Virginia, commented that security measures may have been excessive but that he could not imagine a safer place on the planet than Salt Lake City (Wise, 2002b). Tom Ridge, the director of Homeland Security, echoed Boger, stating in the *New York Times*, "[Salt Lake City] is one of the safest places on the globe. I daresay this is the best plan, the best coordination, the best organized of any Olympics the world has ever seen" (Janofsky, 2002).

Years later, additional insights were uncovered about the securitization of the 2002 Olympic Games. In 2017, the *Associated Press* interviewed whistleblower Thomas Drake, a former top agent for the National Security Agency (NSA) who was assigned to the Salt Lake City Olympics. He revealed: "Officials in the NSA and FBI viewed the Salt Lake Olympics Field Op as a golden opportunity to bring together resources from both agencies to experiment with and fine-tune a new scale of mass surveillance" (Whitehurst, 2017). According to Drake, the NSA's program included the collection of electronic messaging from the area, such as emails and text messages.

The securitization at the Salt Lake City Games sheds light on the broader phenomenon known as National Special Security Events (NSSEs), which are events designated as domestic security threats by the Homeland Security Department because of their significance and vulnerability to terrorist-related activity (Reese, 2021). NSSEs were established by Bill Clinton in 1998 ("National Special Security Events", 2008) and have since become the standard procedure for policing major cultural events, including political conventions and sports mega-events ("Combatting Terrorism: Presidential Decision Directive 62", 1998). The US Secret Service spearheads the coordination of NSSEs, but the Federal Bureau of Intelligence and Federal Emergency Management Agency also assume a prominent role in their organization. The 2002 Olympics were designated as an NSSE, and in addition to the typical agencies, Salt Lake City combined nearly 100 local, federal, and private organizations to manage event security (Bellavita, 2007). The US military also played a central role in securitizing the Olympics despite being historically prohibited from meddling in domestic affairs (Varano et al., 2016, 266). Sports mega-events can initiate long-lasting relationships between militarization and policing tactics in Olympic host cities (Molnar, 2015; see also Cardoso and Pauschinger, this volume). The Olympic state of exception can be deployed to justify intensified security strategies that become the new normal in the wake of the Games.

Soft Power, Sportswashing, and Salt Lake City

The conceptual dimensions of soft power continue to be challenged on several planes. The three debated aspects most relevant to the Salt Lake City Olympics and the invasion of Iraq are the relationship between soft and hard power, the utility of soft power in international relations, and sportswashing's relationship to domestic applications of soft power (Grix & Brannagan, 2016). These features of soft power are amalgamated into the perfect Olympic recipe for disseminating US cultural ideals domestically and internationally, thereby showing the world that despite the terrorist attacks on 9/11, the country remained united, secure, and hegemonic vis-à-vis the international geopolitical system.

Soft and hard power are commonly framed dichotomously. Nonetheless, Joseph Nye recognizes that they can be deployed concurrently; he uses the term "Smart Power" to describe the combination of soft- and hard-power resources that nations have at their disposal, and he claims that successful foreign policy should leverage both types (2008; 2023). The interplay between soft and hard power is more complex than their simultaneous deployment. The mere ownership of hard-power resources can contribute to the effectiveness of a nation's soft-power abilities (Kearn, 2011). Janice Mattern (2005, p. 586) also reasons that soft power's attraction is "sociolinguistically" formed via "representational force," which is a form of coercion, insinuating that soft power may not be so soft. These dynamics were clearly in play in Salt Lake City, where it was sometimes difficult to discern where soft power ended and hard power began. Still, the boundary between soft and hard power remains imprecise, and robust case studies can uncover a variety of dialectical paths and patterns.

As Nye initially designed soft power as a vehicle for international-relations analysis, critics maintain that the theory has a built-in blindspot for domestic audiences. Sven Daniel Wolfe contends there are "[n]ew understandings that can be uncovered by thinking through the domestic aspects of soft power" (2024, p. 5). Sports mega-events spotlight this phenomenon, as when Russia used the 2014 Sochi Olympics to foster the "foundations of an emergent new national identity" (Grix & Kramareva, 2017, p. 2). Jonathan Grix and Barrie Houlihan (2014, p. 575) point to the feel-good phase of sporting mega-events: states frequently utilize national sporting sensations as a guise to promote "domestic and international policy objectives." Wolfe agrees, writing, "The feel-good factor is not necessarily innocent," and states can "create" and "direct" it for "(geo)political purposes" (2024, p. 3). Such socio-political machinations can dovetail with what Kevin Freeman (2012) calls "militaristic swaggering," as mega-events often jumpstart patriotism.

The 2002 Salt Lake City Olympics and its dialectical hard- and soft-power machinations were part of a longer political lineage. Nye (2004, p. 47) notes that, in the context of sport's knack for communicating cultural value, the National Football League's Super Bowl has become an established soft-power vector. Throughout the 1960s, the US government funded the non-profit organization "Sports International" to increase the country's influence in South America (Duckworth & Hunt, 2017). Abdi et al. (2019) found that hosting or participating in local, regional, or international sporting events is one of the most influential sports diplomacy resources for nations wishing to increase soft-power capabilities.

At the Salt Lake City Winter Games, mass media assumed a pivotal role in conveying the United States' power of attraction domestically and internationally. Amid heightened terrorism concerns and the aftermath of 9/11, the 2002 Olympics facilitated a cultural, ideological, and discursive struggle between good versus evil, right versus wrong, and backward versus forward. Security emerged as the crucial objective linking Olympic soft power and the host country's eventual hard-power flex. Atkinson and Young (2002, pp. 68, 69) argue that "[a] 'safe' Games would signal a victory for those committed to fighting terrorism around the world," and as the Olympics proceeded smoothly, the media functioned as a tool of domestic sportswashing while globally trumpeting the power of US "strength, resolve, and hegemony." This mediatized narrative played to national and international audiences while softening the discourse in ways that enabled the 2003 invasion of Iraq.

THE PIVOT FROM SOFT TO HARD POWER AND BACK AGAIN

IOC President Jacques Rogge's statement at the Games' opening ceremony, "We stand united with you in promoting our common ideas and hope for world peace" (Roberts, 2002), swiftly evaporated into vacuous platitude. Less than 400 days after the Salt Lake City Olympics concluded, the United States invaded Iraq, despite worldwide protests against that very prospect.

In the lead-up to the invasion, the rhetoric emanating from Washington, DC, was a striking reminder that the iron fist of hard power often resides inside the velvet glove of soft power. Prominent neoconservatives Lawrence Kaplan and William Kristol (2003, pp. 74, 75) wrote in *The War Over Iraq: Saddam's Tyranny and America's Mission* that the Bush Doctrine staked the right to engage in preemptive, hard-power interventions while simultaneously allowing the United States to "actively promote its principles abroad" such as democracy and freedom. This one-two punch would, they argued, help the United States "remain the world's sole superpower" and promote "American primacy on moral grounds." The Salt Lake City Olympics—and the bundle of soft-power ideals and hard-power threats the Games helped amplify—formed a context that facilitated US military intervention abroad.

The Bush administration's use of soft power vis-à-vis the Olympics did not end in Salt Lake City. After the US invasion of Iraq, "President George W. Bush looked to sport as a rhetorical resource in the war on terrorism," notes discourse scholar Michael Butterworth (2007, p. 185). When the Iraqi men's soccer team went on an improbable run of success at the 2004 Athens Summer Olympics, the Bush administration attempted to capitalize, torquing the team into "a metaphorical embodiment of the war in Iraq, a symbol used by the president on the one hand to trumpet freedom and democracy, and on the other hand to pursue a policy of preemptive war that altered the meanings of both" (Butterworth, 2007, p. 186). In one re-election TV ad, Bush used the team's success to suggest, "Freedom is spreading through the world like a sunrise," with the clear implication that Bush's re-election would harken the spread of freedom and light across the world (Butterworth, 2007, p. 191). On the campaign trail, he took credit for Iraq and Afghanistan's participation in Athens. Someone from Iraq's National Olympic Committee revealed that the United States asked the successful soccer squad to display Afghanistan's flag alongside its own in Athens, although the sports body rejected the idea (Wilkinson, 2004). Rumors circulated that President Bush would fly to Athens if Iraq made it to the gold-medal match (they did not, losing to Paraguay in the semi-final). Bush co-opted soft power in the service of hard power. For historian Abdullah Al-Arian (2022, p. 53), this demonstrated how sport could be "a mode of legitimizing neo-imperial control."

The Bush administration's decision to toggle between soft-power and hard-power strategies generated significant criticism, including from Iraqi soccer players. Iraqi footballer Salih Sadir said, "Iraq as a team does not want Mr. Bush to use us for the presidential campaign," adding, "He can find another way to advertise himself." Teammate Ahmed Manajid asked, "How will [Bush] face his god after having slaughtered so many men and women?" in light of the fact that "he has committed so many crimes" (Wilkinson, 2004). Another Iraqi player said, "I have a message for George Bush: Calm down a little bit. We want to live. Stop killing civilians. Help rebuild Iraq instead of destroying it" (Butterworth, 2007, p. 195).

Al-Arian (2022, pp. 58–59) summarized Bush's soft-power strategy this way: "Having failed to stabilize conditions in Iraq following a war of choice that was deeply divisive, both at home and among US allies in Europe, the Middle East, and elsewhere, the US believed it needed to justify the initial intervention as well as its continued military presence at a moment when the legitimacy of its mission was highly in question." He added, "For the Bush administration, the success of Iraqi athletes was held up as validation of its decision to go to war. The war's defenders pointed to both symbolic and material benefits represented in the Iraqi team's footballing success." Again, we see soft power and hard power bundled into ideology.

Conclusion

The 2002 Salt Lake City Winter Olympics shine a spotlight on the dialectical interplay between soft power and hard power. When considered through a relational epistemology rather than through the crisp causal pathways of positivism, it is clear that the administration of President George W. Bush capitalized off the soft-power attraction value inherent to the mega-event to swerve the United States onto the tundra of hard-power militarization and concomitant bellicosity. Through the tactical machinations of the opening ceremony, replete with Indigenous redwashing and subtle menacing, the Olympics were strategically planned to show a united nation and people. Such unity doubled as grist in support of war and constituted a high-profile link in a historic chain of events where the United States weaponized sport as a soft-power path toward hard-power goals.

The pursuit of soft power chimes with the practice of sportswashing: political leaders use sport as an international legitimation mechanism that also facilitates nationalism while deflecting negative attention from domestic human rights controversies. Sportswashing encourages nationalism and patriotism, and can engender political and economic advancement (Boykoff, 2022; Grix et al., 2023). The Olympics have emerged as a sportswashing battleground where the stakes are high.

The role of mass media is also key to soft-power and sportswashing processes. Atkinson and Young (2002, p. 63) note that the Salt Lake City Olympics "were partly transformed from a celebration of international athletics into a stage for venting and recasting feelings of victimization." This was crucial to ramping up support for subsequent foreign-policy interventions. They add that "in drawing parallels between emotions aroused by terrorist attacks on the United States and the threat of terrorism at the Games, the media assisted in stirring American patriotism, reaffirming cross-national loyalties, and engendering a state of emotional readiness for the 'real' war on terrorism." These discursive ingredients point to three resources that Nye (2004, p. 11) views as vital to soft power: culture, political values, and foreign policies, as rooted in attractiveness and credibility. Soft-power discourses in the context of sports mega-events foster sportswashing, which can entail a "bidirectional" knock-on process that "benefits both the illiberal regimes and the Western sports brands and organizations that collaborate in it" (Grix et al., 2023, p. 16).

The use of soft power as a springboard for hard power can have lasting consequences. The invasions of Iraq and Afghanistan set into motion a "War on Terror" that morphed into different forms under numerous US Presidents, Republican and Democrat alike (Ackerman, 2022). The US "War on Terrorism" has spread far beyond its initial targets—Afghanistan and Iraq—galvanizing pre-existing, racialized tropes about otherized cultures. Brown University's "Costs of War" project estimates that between 2018 and 2020 alone, the United States engaged in what it labeled "counterterrorism" measures in at least 85 countries. The total number of people "killed directly" by violence in places like Afghanistan, Iraq, Pakistan, Syria, and Yemen ranged between 906,000 and 937,000 people. Including indirect deaths, it is closer to 4.5 to 4.6 million people (Brown University, n.d.). That level of violence perpetrated by the US Government is staggering.

The United States is a powerbroker in the Olympic sphere. Los Angeles is hosting the 2028 Summer Olympics, while Salt Lake City is slated to stage the 2034 Winter Games. National Special Security Events, or NSSEs, remain firmly entrenched as the predominant security apparatus meant to protect the Olympic spectacle while simultaneously producing soft power, not unlike an artificial snow cannon, ever more *de rigueur* in the era of climate change, feathering the ski slopes with the fluffy powder that makes the event go. But, as we have seen, sports mega-events can also take nations to distant places in an indirect, relational fashion. Military tactician Carl von Clausewitz famously defined war as "the continuation of policy by other means." A close look at the soft- and hard-power dynamics undergirding the Salt Lake City Games hammers home the notion that sport, too, is politics by other means.

References

Abdi, K., Talebpour, M., Fullerton, J., Ranjkesh, M. J., & Nooghabi, H. J. (2019). Identifying sports diplomacy resources as soft power tools. *Place Branding and Public Diplomacy, 15*(3), 147–155. https://doi.org/10.1057/s41254-019-00115-9

Ackerman, S. (2022). *Reign of terror: How the 9/11 era destabilized America and produced Trump.* Penguin Books.

Al-Arian, A. A. (2022). *Football in the Middle East: State, society, and the beautiful game.* Oxford University Press.

Atkinson, M., & Young, K. (2002). Terror games: Media treatment of security issues at the 2002 Winter Olympic games. *Olympika: The International Journal of Olympic Studies, 11*(1), 53–78.

Bartlett, D. L., & Steele, J. B. (2001, December 10). Snow job. *Sports Illustrated.*

Baxter, S. (2002, February 3). America throws anti-terror net over Winter Olympics. *Sunday Times.*

Bellavita, C. (2007). Changing homeland security: A strategic logic of special event security. *Homeland Security Affairs, 3*, 1. https://www.hsaj.org/articles/140

Boykoff, J. (2022). Toward a theory of sportswashing: Mega-events, soft power, and political conflict. *Sociology of Sport Journal, 39*(4), 342–351. https://doi.org/10.1123/ssj.2022-0095

Brant, M. (2012, February 12). Olympics, Winter Olympics 2002, Olympic Games, Salt Lake City, Utah, Ad Lib, George W. Bush, Olympics speech, International Olympic Committee, IOC, Axis of Evil. *Newsweek.* https://www.newsweek.com/olympics-winter-olympics-2002-olympic-games-salt-lake-city-utah-ad-lib-george-w-bush-olympics-speech

Brown University. (n.d.). *Costs of war.* Watson Institute for International and Public Affairs. https://watson.brown.edu/costsofwar/figures

Butterworth, M. L. (2007). The politics of the pitch: Claiming and contesting democracy through the Iraqi national soccer team. *Communication and Critical/Cultural Studies, 4*(2), 184–203. https://doi.org/10.1080/14791420701296554

Chappelet, J.-L. (2008). *The International Olympic Committee and the Olympic system: The governance of world sport.* Routledge.

Combatting Terrorism: Presidential Decision Directive 62. (1998, May 22). Retrieved October, 25, 2023, from https://irp.fas.org/offdocs/pdd-62.htm

Congelio, B. (2021). Monitoring the policing of Olympic host cities: A novel approach using data analytics and the R programming language. *Journal of Olympic Studies, 2*, 129–145. https://doi.org/10.5406/jofolympstud.2.2.0129

Dubinsky, Y. (2019). From soft power to sports diplomacy: A theoretical and conceptual discussion. *Place Branding and Public Diplomacy, 15*(3), 156–164. https://doi.org/10.1057/s41254-019-00116-8

Duckworth, A., & Hunt, T. M. (2017). Learning the American Way: Sports International and American soft power. *The International Journal of the History of Sport, 34*(11), 1112–1127. https://doi.org/10.1080/09523367.2017.1390452

Fawlty, M. (2002, February 11). Bush makes capital from America's patriot games. *The Australian*.

Freeman, K. (2012). Sport as swaggering: Utilizing sport as soft power. *Sport in Society, 15*(9), 1260–1274. https://doi.org/10.1080/17430437.2012.690403

Gerlach, L. (2008). An uneasy discourse: Salt Lake 2002 and Olympic protest. In *Proceedings: International Symposium for Olympic Research* (pp. 141–151).

Grix, J., & Brannagan, P. M. (2016). Of mechanisms and myths: Conceptualising states' "soft power" strategies through sports mega-events. *Diplomacy & Statecraft, 27*(2), 251–272. https://doi.org/10.1080/09592296.2016.1169791

Grix, J., Dinsmore, A., & Brannagan, P. M. (2023). Unpacking the politics of 'sportswashing': It takes two to Tango. *Politics, 1-22*. https://doi.org/10.1177/02633957231207387

Grix, J., & Houlihan, B. (2014). Sports mega-events as part of a Nation's soft power strategy: The cases of Germany (2006) and the UK (2012). *The British Journal of Politics and International Relations, 16*(4), 572–596. https://doi.org/10.1111/1467-856X.12017

Grix, J., & Kramareva, N. (2017). The Sochi Winter Olympics and Russia's unique soft power strategy. *Sport in Society, 20*(4), 461–475. https://doi.org/10.1080/17430437.2015.1100890

International Olympic Committee. (2001). *Olympic charter: In force as of 4 July 2003*. International Olympic Committee.

Janofsky, M. (2002, January 11). A nation challenged: Casualties and security. *New York Times*.

Kaplan, L. F., & Kristol, W. (2003). *The war over Iraq: Saddam's Tyranny and America's mission*. Encounter Books.

Kearn, D. W. (2011). The hard truths about soft power. *Journal of Political Power, 4*(1), 65–85. https://doi.org/10.1080/2158379X.2011.556869

Knightley, P. (2001, October 4). The disinformation campaign. *The Guardian*. Retrieved November 18, 2023, from https://www.theguardian.com/education/2001/oct/04/socialsciences.highereducation

Leduff, C. (2002, February 14). Olympics: The streets; loitering behind the clean streets. *New York Times*. D1.

Mattern, J. B. (2005). Why 'soft power' isn't so soft: Representational force and the sociolinguistic construction of attraction in world politics. *Millennium, 33*(3), 583–612. https://doi.org/10.1177/03058298050330031601

Millington, R., Giles, A. R., Hayhurst, L. M. C., van Luijk, N., & McSweeney, M. (2019). 'Calling out' corporate redwashing: The extractives industry, corporate social responsibility and sport for development in indigenous communities in Canada. *Sport in Society, 22*(12), 2122–2140. https://doi.org/10.1080/17430437.2019.1567494

Mitchell, G., Duberstein, K., Fehr, D., Cooper Ramo, R., & Benz, J. (1999). *Report of the Special Bid Oversight Commission.* US Senate.

Molnar, A. (2015). The geo-historical legacies of urban security governance and the Vancouver 2010 Olympics. *Geographical Journal, 181*(3), 235–241. https://doi.org/10.1111/geoj.12070

National Special Security Events. (2008, February 9). Retrieved October 25, 2023, from https://web.archive.org/web/20150905055256/http://www.secretservice.gov/nsse.shtml

Nye, J. S. (2004). *Soft power: The means to success in world politics* (1st ed.). Public Affairs.

Nye, J. S. (2008). Public diplomacy and soft power. *The Annals of the American Academy of Political and Social Science, 616*(1), 94–109. https://doi.org/10.1177/0002716207311699

Nye, J. S. (2023). Get smart: Combining hard and soft power. In J. S. Nye (Ed.), *Soft power and great-power competition: Shifting sands in the balance of power between the United States and China* (pp. 63–66). Springer Nature. https://doi.org/10.1007/978-981-99-0714-4_8

Olympic Games to Kick Off; U.S. Troops Inspect Damage of Missile Attack on Suspected al Qaeda Convoy. (2002, February 8). *CNN Wolf Blitzer Reports.* Retrieved October 24, 2023, from http://www.cnn.com/TRANSCRIPTS/0202/08/wbr.02.html.

Reese, S. (2021, January 11). National special security events: Fact sheet. https://crsreports.congress.gov/product/details?prodcode=R43522

Roberts, S. (2002, February 9). Olympics: Opening ceremony; pomp and patriotism at games begins. *New York Times.*

Romney, M. (2004). *Turnaround: Crisis, leadership, and the Olympic Games.* Regnery Pub.

Sanger, D. E. (2002, February 9). Olympics: The President; A perfect time for games, Bush Says. *The New York Times.* Retrieved October 24, 2023, from https://www.nytimes.com/2002/02/09/sports/olympics-the-president-a-perfect-time-for-games-bush-says.html

Springer, S. (2015, April 7). What the Olympics did to my city. *Boston Globe.*

Sullivan, R. (1999). How the Olympics were bought. *Time Magazine, 153*(3). https://content.time.com/time/subscriber/article/0,33009,990075,00.html

The White House. (2002). President Bush opens the 2002 Olympic Games. https://georgewbush-whitehouse.archives.gov/news/releases/2002/02/20020209-2.html

Varano, S. P., Burruss, G. W., & Decker, S. H. (2016). *National special security event* (Salt Lake City 2002). In V. Bajc (Ed.), *Surveilling and securing the Olympics: From Tokyo 1964 to London 2012 and beyond* (pp. 256–274). Palgrave Macmillan UK. https://doi.org/10.1057/9781137290694_13

Wenn, S., Barney, R., & Martyn, S. (2011). *Tarnished rings: The International Olympic committee and the Salt Lake City bid scandal* (Revised ed.). Syracuse University Press.

Whitehurst, L. (2017, June 3). Ex-spy says NSA did mass surveillance during Utah Olympics. *Associated Press News*. Retrieved October 24, 2023, from https://apnews.com/f16a2338b493478cb37b89e86407e316

Wilkinson, T. (2004, August 24). Iraq Olympians say Bush is not on their team. *Los Angeles Times*. https://www.latimes.com/archives/la-xpm-2004-aug-24-fg-iraqiteam24-story.html

Wise, M. (2002a, February 8). Tribes to get their "15 minutes": Presence at Games is both an honor and painful reminder. *New York Times*.

Wise, M. (2002b, February 9). Security: Yes, there's a wait, but for most it is definitely worth it. *New York Times*.

Wolfe, S. D. (2020). 'For the benefit of our nation': Unstable soft power in the 2018 men's World Cup in Russia. *International Journal of Sport Policy and Politics, 12*(4), 545–561. https://doi.org/10.1080/19406940.2020.1839532

Wolfe, S. D. (2024). Introduction: Rationales and foundational concepts. In S. D. Wolfe (Ed.), *The hard edge of soft power: Mega-events, geopolitics, and making nations great again*. Palgrave Macmillan UK.

Open Access This chapter is licensed under the terms of the Creative Commons Attribution 4.0 International License (http://creativecommons.org/licenses/by/4.0/), which permits use, sharing, adaptation, distribution and reproduction in any medium or format, as long as you give appropriate credit to the original author(s) and the source, provide a link to the Creative Commons license and indicate if changes were made.

The images or other third party material in this chapter are included in the chapter's Creative Commons license, unless indicated otherwise in a credit line to the material. If material is not included in the chapter's Creative Commons license and your intended use is not permitted by statutory regulation or exceeds the permitted use, you will need to obtain permission directly from the copyright holder.

CHAPTER 10

Conclusion: After the Spotlight

Sven Daniel Wolfe

Abstract This conclusion briefly revisits the preceding chapters, drawing out common themes and proposing some questions for future research. Each chapter used mega-events to explore the internal dynamics of host societies after the global spotlight, investigating the implications of hosting on a variety of publics. Brought into comparative perspective, the chapters reveal a global community of host cities and societies, each suffering from similar broken promises and squandered potential. Regarding future research, the conclusion underscores the importance of local context, attention to difference, and the role of time, restating the book's overall dedication to exploring beneath the glittering Potemkin surface of these perpetually popular but perniciously problematic mega-events.

Keywords Soft power • Potemkinism • Geopolitics • Time • Mega-events

S. D. Wolfe (✉)
ETH Zürich, Zurich, Switzerland

Institute of Geography, University of Neuchâtel, Neuchâtel, Switzerland
e-mail: swolfe@ethz.ch

Mega-events are still something of a common currency in our increasingly fractured and fragile world. They come with seasonal regularity and are almost universally recognizable, providing opportunities for celebration, relaxation, and potential communion with neighbors from down the street or the other side of the globe. But this presentation is incomplete. As demonstrated in these chapters, the lofty goals and sanitized imaginaries presented by organizers and boosters do not fully reflect local realities. Too often with mega-events, the spectacle and glamor eclipse all else, rendering invisible the actual impacts on host cities and societies. Combined with the fact that most scholarly and media attention disappears after the closing ceremonies, this means that the Potemkin presentation can pass into history as the full story.

This book works against these tendencies and strives for a more complete retelling of the aftereffects of hosting. These chapters return past mega-events to the spotlight, exploring underneath the superficial surface to reveal a more complicated picture of how authorities and governments attempt to direct mega-event soft power toward a variety of audiences, how these attempts are imbricated with hard power realities, and what effects they engender on host cities and societies.

Despite important regional variations, the cases collected here share much in common. Reading the book as a whole reveals something like a global community of former host societies, all of whom shared in the decidedly mixed bag of bringing the world to their front yard. What happens in the back yard during that process is both unique to each case and recognizable across former host cities worldwide.

As these are global events, the book features cases from each major global region. Clearly there are problems and exclusions with this approach (Why China and not Japan or South Korea? Why the United Kingdom instead of France or Germany?). At the same time, the goal was not to be comprehensive—how could we be?—but rather to provide a more-or-less global overview that attempts to strike a healthy balance between depth and breadth. Each author in this global team is expert in their region, thus providing the depth. The breadth comes when they are brought into comparative perspective with sister cases from around the world. Future work should attempt to fill the gaps overlooked here, both empirically and theoretically. Might there be cases in an unmentioned country—perhaps with a middle-tier mega-event—where the theoretical purchase of Potemkinism falls flat, or where the soft power potential is actualized without a hard edge?

10 CONCLUSION: AFTER THE SPOTLIGHT   147

Taken together, these chapters reveal the local articulations of global processes that follow recognizable patterns, and with remarkably similar effects. For instance, hosts in developing regions tend to try leveraging mega-events for international recognition, while those in more established economies typically strive for refreshed political relevance combined with some degree of urban revitalization or renewal. In both cases, though, these internationally focused aspirations too often result in deleterious outcomes for host populations. There are many such patterns on display in this book.

Though the chapters differ in their choice of scope and focus, just as the authors themselves belong to different disciplinary traditions, I find the work complementary rather than contradictory—providing corroborating evidence, filling in the gaps, or suggesting alternative approaches to certain aspects of other chapters. Consider the broken promises for the Cape Town residents relayed by Musikavanhu in parallel with Cardoso and Pauschinger's work on Rio de Janeiro. Despite the fact that they do not focus on Brazilian resident experience—instead drawing links between mega-events and the militarization of security practices—the theme of broken promises runs like an undercurrent through this chapter. Every investment into the new security centers is an investment not made into meaningful social or material advancements for the host population.

Going further, take the real estate speculation underlying the hosting experiences in Brisbane as detailed by Holleran, Minner, and Abbott, demonstrating how local power constellations use mega-events to legitimize or force through controversial plans at the municipal level. This work encourages thinking about similar processes in other host cities, regardless of the fact that the other authors do not explicitly engage this specific aspect. Nevertheless, a cursory look at other literature reveals that real estate speculation plays a central role in the broader mega-event story and reminds that these disparate processes are all of a piece. Similarly, Whigham's exploration of internal and external (geo)political dynamics in the United Kingdom highlights dysfunctional constitutional arrangements that are both brought to light and papered over by hosting. This Potemkin presentation of UK unity parallels Gurol's analysis of the Chinese party-state's image projection in Beijing 2008 and 2022, and suggests that— regardless of political-economic context—hosting mega-events can enable authoritarian practices and run counter to domestic realities and authentic democratic processes.

Consider further how the mega-event presentation of unity affected the muscular posture of the United States after the 9/11 terrorist attacks, elaborated by Boykoff and McFeely. Kazakov and Andrejevs detail striking connections here with the Central and Eastern European mega-event experience, including the mega-event decade in Russia. Despite the disastrous aftereffects—the ultimate consolidation of authoritarian power and the war against Ukraine—the initial motivations for hosting aimed to introduce better relations between Russia and the wider world. These national attempts to participate in the global "big leagues" dovetail with mega-events in Qatar, explored by Zumbraegel and Sons. That chapter highlights the importance of key individuals in the articulation of the mega-event, which resonates with developments in Brazil and beyond. Similarly, as mega-events will be hosted more often in the Gulf region, it is important to remember the particular risks of entrenched authoritarian functioning elaborated in other chapters.

There are so many intricate webs of connection between the cases. Consider the Command-and-Control System established in Brazil and compare with the new systems of surveillance and control established in Sochi and then Russia as a whole. These resonate in uncomfortable ways with the securitization and militarization processes seen in Salt Lake City 2002 and London 2012, and remind that contexts nominally considered democratic and free are not immune from the spread of authoritarian practices.

None of this is to say that these mega-event stories are commensurate, particularly in regard to resident experience. Further, we should not be tempted into a competitive analysis and attempt to rank these stories in a kind of Olympics of Suffering. Rather, the point with the comparative perspective is to appreciate how these chapters harmonize with one another, suggesting new avenues for investigation of shared or contrasted experience.

To conclude this collection, I want to explore some connections, questions, and overarching themes revealed by reading the chapters as a collective work. First, difference matters. To start, the uniqueness of each host city and country affects profoundly the articulation of the mega-event. This seems self-evident but it is worth unpacking the implications. Mega-events always involve significant opportunity costs no matter where in the world they are, but the impacts tend to hit harder in developing economies—as detailed, for example, in Musikavanhu's chapter on South Africa. To be sure, no country's elites are immune to the temptation of leveraging mega-event soft power on the world stage, but it is important to remember that the deleterious impacts tend to be felt more severely in some economies over others.

More broadly, the base conditions (political functioning, economic structure, cultural specificities) of different host societies bring to light different potentials within the mega-event experience. For instance, there seems to be a strange proclivity for authoritarianism within mega-event planning. If the host society also leans toward authoritarian practices, then these tendencies can complement and augment one another. Cardoso and Pauschinger demonstrate this in their chapter on the authoritarian legacy in Brazil, as do Zumbraegel and Sons in their investigation of power players in Qatar. Similarly, if the host society is undergoing a shift to more neoliberal functioning, this can resonate with parallel affinities in the mega-event and shape planning priorities to match. Holleran, Minner, and Abbott explore this in the real estate speculation and tourism-focused reorientation of Brisbane, just as Whigham does on the neoliberal political orthodoxy underlying mega-events in the United Kingdom. The larger conclusion is that mega-events should not be studied without appropriate attention to the already existing conditions of their hosts. They do not, after all, take place in a vacuum. This is especially important now that mega-event reforms—under the laudable but potentially Potemkin goal of sustainability—have refashioned hosting requirements to work in concert with a city's existing plans.

Each of these chapters tackles a particular aspect of difference, for instance focusing on different actors involved in the mega-event story. By nature, mega-events are elite projects, and elite actors in any host nation commonly attempt to leverage them for their own aims, whether longstanding or new. Insofar as these aims overlap with the public good, then mega-events can be said to be beneficial. At the same time, it is clear that mega-events cause harm, and that this harm disproportionately affects the poorest and most vulnerable. In between these categories is a broad swath of host city residents who are not involved formally in the event, nor who are particularly damaged by it. It is here that the feel-good effect is most powerful. Outside of the host city, this can also affect global audiences who tune in, including assemblages of international business, media, and political figures, to say nothing of the academics and other commentators who also make their living in the wider ecosystem of this traveling circus. This international audience is the basis for what is understood as mega-event soft power. One of the core contentions of this book is that soft power can be directed at different audiences, both international and domestic. The larger point is that a sensitivity to the differences between and within these multiple audiences is key to understanding why the meaning of mega-events can vary so widely.

There is another dimension of difference that plays a crucial role: that of time. The *when* of the question is understudied and too often unexamined. This does not only apply to the host country, which—given the time frames involved in mega-event planning—is substantially a different place than the country that won the bid. Time also applies to the study of mega-events, where most can be divided roughly into *before* or *after* the Games, with a minority concentrating on *during*. Time can also refer both to the specific period under investigation and to when the piece itself was written, as both have implications for results. For instance, a piece written during the early phases of the preparatory period, when hosting seems full of promise, can differ wildly from a piece written during the later phases, as organizers scramble to complete projects on time, and the city roils under the scramble of last-minute preparations. Similarly, a post-event analysis taken six months after the closing might reveal an array of unused venues, but several years later these might be fully occupied and playing important roles in the city. Another question to consider is how long the feel-good effect lasts, and how this might change common understandings of the value of hosting. The point is that a sensitivity to the differences engendered by time is vital for a more complete understanding of what mega-events do to cities and societies. For this reason, the authors here work broadly on the aftereffects period, or more bluntly, within the hangover phase of the mega-event story. This is not only due to the relative lack of studies written after the peak of global attention, but also to provide a counterweight to the power of the feel-good effect.

In sum, mega-event scholarship relies on abstraction in order to explore mega-event phenomena—whether regarding the synecdoche of nations or cities, the homogenization of actor groups, or the nature of time. In so doing we risk mistaking the abstraction for reality and thereby miss the complexity of actually existing relationships. In this light it is crucial to remember that nothing—no group and indeed not even an individual—is homogenous, and that thinking in categories is a useful analytical shortcut but not all there is. In a variety of different ways, the authors collected here strive to defy categorical thinking and unsettle the research on mega-events. The chapters—organized according to emphasis on Potemkinism, engagement with authoritarian practices, and relationship to hard power—could easily have been sorted in different ways to emphasize other aspects of the work. In all cases, however, the authors use mega-events to explore the internal dynamics of host societies after the spotlight, unpacking elite planning priorities and investigating the implications of hosting on a variety of publics.

Within this frame, the authors explore multiple dimensions of mega-event soft power. Here it is important to differentiate between soft power *targets* (whether international or domestic) and soft power *byproduct effects*. In other words, aside from their putative goals, soft power projects can engender a variety of unintended effects on different populations. Reading these chapters as a whole, a new feature of Potemkinism occurs to me: perhaps Potemkinism is the domestic byproduct from internationally targeted soft power. In any case, the chapters each reveal different interpretation of this relationship, whether focusing on the display of national significance for the international stage while masking problematic domestic affairs (Gurol; Whigham; Holleran, Minner, and Abbott), the hard power aspirations hiding under the façade of sporting unity (Kazakov and Andrejevs; Boykoff and McFeely), the spectacular celebrations that conceal the growth and entrenchment of authoritarian practices (Zumbraegel and Sons; Cardoso and Pauschinger), or the efforts to introduce a more palatable national image while deemphasizing authentic domestic improvements (Musikavanhu; Kazakov and Andrejevs).

These are complicated questions that have worldwide relevance. They also suggest numerous potential avenues for future research. Can hosting mega-events in more closed or repressive societies help inculcate more humane politics? Or does hosting simply offer a smokescreen for political consolidation and greed, while granting already powerful figures a global stage on which to project superficial images of the nation? Is there ever any place for marginalized populations in mega-events, and where is the line between inclusion and tokenism? Can mega-events ever be divorced from their destructive tendencies, or are the ideas of reform merely cover for the continuation of business as usual, albeit in more disguised and diffuse forms? I do not suggest that there are clear answers to these questions. Rather, as demonstrated by the chapters collected here, the point is to penetrate the mega-event spectacle and investigate what hides underneath the glittering Potemkin surface.

This book reveals that certain aspects of the mega-event story remain consistent, regardless of local conditions. These are major investments for host societies, and they should be taken seriously as political and economic projects with high risks. Insofar as possible, discourse should be removed from the intoxication of glamor and prestige, and we—researchers and residents alike—should remain wary of hyperbolic and utopian promises. This can be a real challenge in the whirlwind euphoria of the feel-good effect.

Soft power is no joke. There is profound potential to move societies via the emotional and affective dimensions of hosting, which is not to be dismissed lightly. Domestically, soft power can be coopted into nationalism and aggression, but it can equally contribute to life-changing feelings of togetherness, belonging, and a greater purpose. Internationally, it can alter the trajectory of entire nations, opening or closing states to wider circuits of commerce, tourism, and social and cultural interchange. But, too often, these projects generate nasty byproduct side-effects, or this potential for better and more meaningful relations is squandered. Instead of opener societies, better international and domestic connections, higher standards of living, and a global party for the benefit of all, we see the same sad results of the same tired mega-event story. In the end, the logic of the profit motive tends to dominate other considerations and possibilities. Under the pressure of presenting prestige in the glare of the international gaze, mega-event preparations too often are accomplished for the checkmark, rather than substantially improving conditions for host cities and societies. In too many cases, we see that hosting mega-events lands on the backs of those least able to afford them. It is an open question as to why local organizers and authorities regularly mortgage the future of their most vulnerable citizens.

In hopes of steering toward better outcomes, this book explores mega-events after the spotlight to unpack what they have done to cities and societies worldwide. How they use sport to restructure internal political dynamics, and how they use passion and prestige to hide terrible consequences. How they reveal dynamics unique to each host context, and how they ignore local voices in every city around the globe. How they play into geopolitical aspiration, and how they play out to the disadvantage of the poor and vulnerable. How they are perennially popular, yet how they mask their problems under a Potemkin surface of superlatives, spectacle, and success. Together, these chapters present an international and transdisciplinary understanding of the local and global (geo)political implications of hosting mega-events, ultimately revealing the hard edge hiding within the allure of soft power.

Open Access This chapter is licensed under the terms of the Creative Commons Attribution 4.0 International License (http://creativecommons.org/licenses/by/4.0/), which permits use, sharing, adaptation, distribution and reproduction in any medium or format, as long as you give appropriate credit to the original author(s) and the source, provide a link to the Creative Commons license and indicate if changes were made.

The images or other third party material in this chapter are included in the chapter's Creative Commons license, unless indicated otherwise in a credit line to the material. If material is not included in the chapter's Creative Commons license and your intended use is not permitted by statutory regulation or exceeds the permitted use, you will need to obtain permission directly from the copyright holder.

GPSR Compliance

The European Union's (EU) General Product Safety Regulation (GPSR) is a set of rules that requires consumer products to be safe and our obligations to ensure this.

If you have any concerns about our products, you can contact us on ProductSafety@springernature.com

In case Publisher is established outside the EU, the EU authorized representative is:

Springer Nature Customer Service Center GmbH
Europaplatz 3
69115 Heidelberg, Germany

Batch number: 08442663

Printed by Printforce, the Netherlands